SHAKESPEARE'S TRAGEDIES
ALL THAT MATTERS

*In memory of our parents Cliff and Rhiannon James,
Jack and Norah Scott – always remembered,
with love and thanks.*

SHAKESPEARE'S TRAGEDIES

Michael Scott

ALL THAT MATTERS

First published in Great Britain in 2015 by Hodder and Stoughton. An Hachette UK company.
This edition published in 2015 by John Murray Learning

British Library Cataloguing in Publication Data: a catalogue record for this title is available from the British Library.

Library of Congress Catalog Card Number: on file

Paperback ISBN 9781444189926

eBook ISBN 9781444189940

10 9 8 7 6 5 4 3 2 1

The publisher has used its best endeavours to ensure that any website addresses referred to in this book are correct and active at the time of going to press. However, the publisher and the author have no responsibility for the websites and can make no guarantee that a site will remain live or that the content will remain relevant, decent or appropriate.

The publisher has made every effort to mark as such all words which it believes to be trademarks. The publisher should also like to make it clear that the presence of a word in the book, whether marked or unmarked, in no way affects its legal status as a trademark.

Every reasonable effort has been made by the publisher to trace the copyright holders of material in this book. Any errors or omissions should be notified in writing to the publisher, who will endeavour to rectify the situation for any reprints and future editions.

Typeset by Cenveo® Publisher Services.

Printed and bound in Great Britain by CPI Group (UK) Ltd., Croydon, CR0 4YY.

John Murray Learning policy is to use papers that are natural, renewable and recyclable products and made from wood grown in sustainable forests. The logging and manufacturing processes are expected to conform to the environmental regulations of the country of origin.

Hodder & Stoughton Ltd
Carmelite House
50 Victoria Embankment
London EC4Y 0DZ
www.hodder.co.uk

Also available in ebook

Contents

Preface

What is it that matters about Shakespearean tragedy and in particular the four great tragedies: *Hamlet*, *Macbeth*, *King Lear*, *Othello*? Perhaps that tragedy exposes in one form or another, from one ideological viewpoint or another, issues relating to individual identity within or as framed by the society which produces it and participates in it as performer, reader, student, actor or audience.

Through the genre of tragedy Shakespeare poses many questions which he does not answer. It is the questioning which matters, challenging us to enter a dialogue with each play, its author and others who have encountered the tragedies down the centuries. The approach here to entering this dialogue is similar to that in the companion volume on *Shakespeare's Comedies*. We do not ask what the tragedies mean, we ask how they work. Through an understanding of the mechanics of the plays and the art of the playwright, we engage with the questions contained in the plays. Different meanings emerge depending on the predilictions of the audience or reader, or the artistic vision within the corporate and collective experience of a theatrical performance. It is this malleability which ensures the plays' continuing success.

Quotations from the works are taken from *The RSC Shakespeare: The Complete Works*, edited by Jonathan Bate and Eric Rasmussen (Basingstoke: Macmillan, paperback edition, 2008), and based on the First Folio (1623).

1

Introduction: Shakespeare and tragedy

Remember the life of these things consists in action.

John Marston, *'To My Equal Reader'*, The Fawn *(1604–6)*

Shakespeare's plays, particularly his tragedies, resonate with antecedents in Roman and Greek theatre. Neoclassical criticism has traditionally defined the structure of tragedy and applied it from Greek tragedy to Shakespeare. In such readings drama depends on conflict, and the plot of the play is as a knot which the dramatic action proceeds to unravel. The structure, however, is like a pyramid. This has exposition, rising action, climax, falling action, catastrophe.

Structure is important. Shakespeare was aware of the Roman Seneca, but he may not have been so familiar with the Greeks Aeschylus, Sophocles or Euripides. Nevertheless, the main plot of *Hamlet*, for example, can be related to the classical structure described above. In such a reading, the climax of the play, the turning point, is when Hamlet fails to kill Claudius at prayer (Act 3 Scene 3). The plot rises to this point and then falls towards the catastrophe, the deaths in Act 5 of Hamlet and several others. The problem with this definition, however, is that Greek tragedy is also tied to the classical notion of 'the unities': the three unities derived from Aristotle's *Poetics* implied that the duration of the dramatic action must take place in a single day (Time), in a single location (Place), and must contain a single plot (Action). For Aristotle, 'character' was a secondary device, an instrument used to carry the 'plot' of the action.

Neither *Hamlet* nor the other Shakespearean tragedies conform to this strict model. In *Hamlet*, Shakespeare spreads the action over a much longer time span and the play has a series of parallels and sub-plots involving, for example, Fortinbras, Ophelia and Laertes, all of whom have lost their father and are portrayed as coping with their loss in different ways. So the sub-plots are parallel plots: Fortinbras threatens the Danish throne; Ophelia, it is suggested, commits suicide; Laertes' rebellion, prompted by the death of his father, is turned by Claudius into a form of revenge, which is then folded into a larger plot engineered by Claudius to protect his own position as king. This is one of many forms of repetition in the play, all of which expand the material of the main plot and increase the complexity of the action.

Despite the image of a pyramid, the imposition of the traditional structure is defeated by the complexity of the plot. Some 20th-century critics, most notably Northrop

▲ A medieval illustration of the wheel of Fortune, showing the rise and fall of individuals of all levels of society.

Frye, have offered alternatives, Frye discerning six phases of tragedy, moving from "the heroic to the ironic"[1] and five 'modes' or 'categories' integral to tragedy. It must be doubtful that Shakespeare worked in this way, and I prefer to look at a less complex structure underlying the four great tragedies, and to organize the action of these plays in terms of the following themes.

1 **Problems:** are set which relate directly to the protagonist, who must be of significant standing in the social order, but the problems may affect that social order by involving more than just the protagonist or a single plot. In the opening scenes of each of the four great tragedies more than one problem is described, and although there is a central narrative, integrated sub-plots are developed that contribute to the pattern of the play. This allows a play to be the sum of its parts rather than to follow a single linear narrative line dependent on the 'character' of the protagonist.

2 **Journeys:** the solutions to the problems involve the protagonist and other characters who undertake mental journeys. This may also involve geographical relocations, which expose ambitions or anxieties.

3 **Arrivals:** during these mental and/or physical journeys, self-enquiry leads those with ambitions or anxieties to arrive at some form of self-knowledge, found in recognition scenes.

4 **Complications** arise which may postpone the path from self-recognition to satisfactory resolution.

5 Silence: through the death of the protagonist (and sometimes his antagonist) is the usual result.

So in *Hamlet*, for example, this basic five-part structure emerges as follows.

1 The problems initially set at the beginning of the play relate to the death of King Hamlet, exemplified by the Ghost's revelations concerning the "incestuous" marriage of the queen to the late king's brother, Claudius, who has committed fratricide in order to achieve his ambitions. But there is a second, more pressing political problem that endangers the new king's regime: the threat to Denmark of an attack by the Norwegians, led by young Fortinbras, whose father was killed in combat by King Hamlet.

2 Hamlet embarks on a 'journey' to test the veracity of the Ghost's claims, and he determines, on the instruction of the Ghost, to solve the problem by vengeance at whatever cost. He also embarks on a psychological journey since the events in Denmark appear to disturb his mental equilibrium. The new king sends emissaries to the king of Norway in order to avoid invasion and, with the queen, attempts to appease her malcontent son.

3 The king's emissaries return having secured peace, but for Hamlet various actions occur, including a brief moment of introspection from Claudius and Hamlet's chastising of his mother. At this meeting Polonius is accidentally killed and this leads to Hamlet being forced to take a physical journey not of his own choosing, from which when he returns, he asserts his identity, "This is I,/Hamlet the Dane" (5.1.210–11).

4 A further complication occurs with the return from Paris of Laertes, determined to revenge the death of his father, Polonius. His sister Ophelia's lapse into madness and ultimate 'suicide' adds further impetus to Laertes' desire for revenge, and this is exploited by Claudius.

5 These 'plots' all come together in the final act of the play, and the silence comes through multiple deaths, including Hamlet's own. At the end, Hamlet acknowledges Fortinbras' entitlement to the throne of Denmark: "he has my dying voice" (5.2.305). Hamlet dies with the words "The rest is silence." (307)

▶ What is 'tragedy'?

Having considered the structure of tragic plays, we might ask what 'tragedy' is. Traditionally critics look back to the classical stage and to Aristotle, who wrote:

> *Tragedy is an imitation of an action that is admirable, complete and possesses magnitude; in language made pleasurable, each of its species separated in different parts; performed by actors, not through narration; effecting through pity and fear the purification (purgation) of such emotions.*[2]

This concept refers to the emotional state in which the audience finds itself at the completion of the tragic action. Through the play, feelings of pity and terror are created in the spectators, and at the end those emotions are released, purged, purified and brought back into balance. This release (*catharsis*) can allow the audience to feel elated at what they have witnessed while simultaneously relieved that they experience the tragedy vicariously through the fate of the protagonist. The protagonist, the main character in the play, is usually someone of high rank who suffers a reversal of fortune, sometimes brought about by his own pride (*hubris*) and his refusal to compromise. He is blind to the consequences of his pride and the actions that lead to his downfall, but towards the end of the play there is a moment of recognition (*anagnorisis*) in which the blindness is lifted and he achieves a modicum of self-knowledge that comes too late for him to avoid the consequences of his actions. Thus in the face of defeat the protagonist reveals admirable human qualities, something that led the critic A. C. Bradley to lament the inconsolable sense of 'waste' that we are left with at the end of the tragic action[3].

In Shakespearean tragedy, the recognition scene is thought to be as poignant as in Greek drama, as, for example, in *King Lear* Act 4 when the king 'discovers' the magnitude of his errors. *Anagnorisis*, or discovery, begins with the king articulating his pain, "but I am bound/Upon a wheel of fire"; then he confesses his confusion, "Where have I been? Where am I? Fair daylight?/I am mightily abused"; and finally he acknowledges his own frailty, confessing the foolishness of his age as he recognizes Cordelia, the daughter whom he has wronged:

> *Pray do not mock me:*
> *I am a very foolish fond old man,*
> *Fourscore and upward, not an hour more nor less,*

> ... *Do not laugh at me,*
> *For, as I am a man, I think this lady*
> *To be my child Cordelia.*

Cordelia answers simply, "And so I am, I am." (4.6.62f.)

In many productions this is a highly charged emotional and cathartic moment and one which 18th-century critics would have wished to see as the natural end to the play. But Shakespeare frustrates this desire by producing further, harrowing complications. The play follows through the consequences of Lear's errors by producing further calamities and the result is the death of Cordelia, following Lear's recognition of her quality. In Act 5 Lear is left with nothing but death as he holds the lifeless body of his youngest daughter in his arms:

> *Why should a dog, a horse, a rat have life,*
> *And thou no breath at all? Thou'lt come no more,*
> *Never, never, never, never, never!*
> *Pray you undo this button: thank you, sir,*
> *Do you see this? Look on her, look, her lips,*
> *Look there, look there!* [*He dies.*] (5.3.323–8)

Does this intensify the cathartic effect that criticism teaches us is appropriate at the ending of a tragedy, or does it frustrate our expectations of the play? To Nahum Tate (1652–1715), and Samuel Johnson (1704–84), it was beyond the realms of sensibility or decorum. In 1681, Tate adapted the play, cutting out the final act and producing a happy ending in which the protagonist and Cordelia remain alive. This was the only version of the play performed until the 1820s.

For 20th- and 21st-century audiences, Shakespeare's original ending has come to express the vacuity of existence and the violent barbarism of contemporary experience. In its structural form, *King Lear* debates other classical themes, such as the nature and purpose of divine intervention or retribution (*nemesis*), which comes in the form of divine punishment for human error – as in Gloucester's horrifying blinding, which leads paradoxically to his 'insight' into his own plight ("As flies to wanton boys are we to th'gods:/They kill us for their sport": 4.1.41–2) – or reversals of fortune (*peripeteia*), such as when the villain Edmund seeks to halt the execution of Cordelia but the letter of pardon arrives too late to prevent her death. Some modern critics have credited Shakespeare with pushing the genre much further in depicting the vacuous bleakness of existence in the face of the finality of death. In Act 1, King Lear foreshadows what is to come when he instructs Cordelia that "Nothing will come of nothing: speak again" (1.1.82). Act 5 ends in the silence of their deaths, echoing, perhaps, the irony of Hamlet's final words, "The rest is silence" (5.2.307).

For much of the 20th century, A. C. Bradley's views provided a philosophical basis for the concept of Shakespeare's tragedy. In contradiction of Aristotle, who held that "Tragedy is not an imitation of persons, but of actions and of life"[4], Bradley insisted on the primacy of character. He pointed towards the unity of feelings in the plays and he saw the structure of the plays as mirroring what is known as a Hegelian dialectic, in which a thesis and an antithesis come into conflict with each other but a resolution occurs by a synthesis of the two at a higher level, which constitutes the close of the play. In this analysis of Shakespeare's tragedies, two polarities expressing good and evil each destroy one another in order to produce a new situation. For Bradley, character is the determining factor, while for Aristotle it is "the events, i.e. the plot, [that] are what tragedy is there for, and that is the most important thing of all"[5].

As the 20th century progressed, critics began to challenge Bradley's approach to Shakespeare. In a famous essay[6], L. C. Knights exposed the absurdity of thinking of Shakespeare's characters as having an independent and individual life outside the play. He insisted, however, on the close examination and appreciation of the language of the plays, although he widened this critical emphasis to take into account historical, social and political issues[7]. Such issues have grown in importance and have, in contemporary criticism, challenged Aristotelian notions of tragedy and the way in which we regard the plays. In a seminal work that in 1980 inaugurated a new critical school of thought known as New Historicism, Stephen Greenblatt called for an emphasis on the literary text in its social and cultural context. He directed attention towards language as the primary means of accessing and shaping "the world".

> *Language, like other sign systems, is a collective construction; our interpretive task must be to grasp more sensitively the consequences of this fact by investigating both the social presence to the world of the literary text and the social presence of the world in the literary text.*[8]

The twenty years from the 1980s onwards was a time of heated debate and discussion. New Historicist critics saw the need to locate dramatic texts in the culture of their original creation in terms that Greenblatt advocated, but this was taken further by more politically conscious critics, the Cultural Materialists, who drew on a long tradition of Marxist and socialist thought. The Cultural Materialists questioned the fundamental emphasis placed by Bradley and others upon 'character' in tragedy. They preferred to look at 'subjectivity' and the social pressures under which it was produced. Following from the Marxist rejection of the notion of the 'individual' that had informed the characterization of the tragic protagonist for so long, emphasis was now placed upon how the protagonist was 'produced'. Jonathan Dollimore, for example, insisted on a Marxist materialistic interpretation of the individual: "It is not the consciousness of men that determines their being, but, on the contrary, their social being that determines their consciousness"[9].

The Cultural Materialists found considerable support in the writings of theatre dramatists and theoreticians such as Bertolt Brecht, Antonin Artaud, Jan Kott and Augusto Boal from the 1930s onwards, and in the practice of influential theatre directors such as Peter Brook and Peter Hall from the 1960s onwards. Boal in particular attacked the concept of the tragic flaw (*hamartia*) and saw the retribution it provokes in traditional concepts of tragedy as a method of re-enforcing social control. In his view, tragedy creates a means of sacrificing the protagonist in order to guarantee conformity to the prevailing social ethos. Thus the whole notion of catharsis is represented as being politically coercive. The critical debate between Liberal Humanists and Cultural Materialists continues within literary and political circles[10].

Cultural Materialists might question the notion of the individual, but a sense of individuality emerged in European thought during the Renaissance. In traditional Christianity, authority had been located in the institution of the Church, whose task it was to mediate and to legitimize scriptural meaning, until the Renaissance brought challenges to the Church's authority. Humanism, developed at first in 14th-century Italy, was disseminated throughout Europe in the 15th and 16th centuries, fostered by the advent of printing and the growth in reading that it facilitated. The movement encouraged a return to original sources and religious reflection, so access to 'the new thinking' gave individuals a greater opportunity for personal interpretation. This trend was further developed by Protestantism generally after the Reformation and in the newly established Church in England, although in England certain elements of traditional religious thinking remained. These events coincided with – indeed, largely facilitated – developments in science that resulted in a radical rethinking of the organization of the universe, the whole creating a tension between a perceived innate human capacity to shape existence, and a concept of a divine power that could shape our ends. It was this historical confluence of cultural and religious ideas that influenced the development of the kind of tragedy that we associate with Shakespeare. But that does not imply that we should define the genre in classical or neoclassical terms, nor in terms associated with Christian or liberal humanism. My discussion of the four tragedies will consider how the plays may have worked within the context of the influences pertaining at the time of their inception, and of how they may also work in a modern context.

Elizabethan tragedy

Traditionally, Elizabethan tragedy has been defined as being of three types: *de casibus*, which shows the rise and fall of a great individual; *revenge tragedy*, which places the individual within a corrupt society failing to find justice through legal or religious institutions and thereby resorting to acts of personal vengeance; and *domestic tragedy*, as exemplified in plays such as the anonymous *Arden of Feversham* (c.1592), which deal with issues that are implicitly rather than explicitly political but that nevertheless have some links with the development and progress of the plays under discussion. In one sense *King Lear* demonstrates a domesticity which has far-reaching public and hence political implications. Given the modern separation of the spheres of 'public' and 'private', we have to ask ourselves to what extent the domestic impinges upon the political and vice versa.

▶ The text: which text?

In order to try to avoid difficulties or solve problems about a play's meaning, it is sometimes said that we should simply go back to the original text. This, however, is not easy. The plays were not intended as literary artefacts but as scripts for performance. It appears that Shakespeare did not oversee the printing of his works;

although some of them were published in his lifetime, others were not. The result is that for some of the plays we have a number of early texts which differ from one another. The modern texts we read are often compilations of a number of early scripts. In *The Oxford Shakespeare: Complete Works* (1988), editors Stanley Wells and Gary Taylor decided to publish two versions of *King Lear* from different 'originals': *The History of King Lear* from the 1608 Quarto and *The Tragedy of King Lear* from the First Folio (1623). Plays are dynamic and changes are made through rehearsal, through performance, through revival and also through theft, as is the case with *Hamlet*. Possibly Shakespeare's best-known tragedy and most quoted play, *Hamlet* first appeared in print in 1603 in a quarto-sized edition known now as Q1 and often referred to as the 'bad Quarto'. It was published again in a 1604/05 quarto edition, known as Q2 or sometimes as the 'good Quarto'. It was published again after his death by two of Shakespeare's fellow actors, John Heminges and Henry Condell, in the first collected edition of Shakespeare's plays, the First Folio in 1623.

Why is there a 'bad' Quarto and a 'good' Quarto? There were no copyright laws in Shakespeare's time. Consequently his company, the Lord Chamberlain's Men, which later became the King's Men, did not rush to publish plays in performance since they did not want rival companies to steal and make money from the scripts. Actors might move from one company to another having memorized major parts of a popular play. Members of the audience or a rival company's actors may have tried to memorize particular parts of the play. The result might not only be a rival production but also the publication of an unauthorized, incorrect version of the play. This is what may have happened with the 1603 version of *Hamlet*.

To give an indication of how the Q1 version differs from the Folio, in Q1 (the 'bad Quarto'), Hamlet's most famous soliloquy begins:

> *To be, or not to be, I there's the point,*
> *To Die, to sleepe, is that all? I all:*
> *No, to sleepe, to dreame, I mary there it goes ...*[11]

Compare it with that of the First Folio:

> *To be or not to be, that is the question:*
> *Whether 'tis nobler in the mind to suffer*
> *The slings and arrows of outrageous fortune,*
> *Or to take arms against a sea of troubles,*
> *And by opposing end them? To die, to sleep –*
> *No more ...*
> >   *To die, to sleep:*
> *To sleep, perchance to dream: ay, there's the rub,*
> (3.1.62–7, 70–1)

The texts of Shakespeare's plays that we read or produce today are interpretative texts, compiled by modern editors who make choices usually, and when alternatives exist, from the Quarto editions and the First Folio, although sometimes they produce an edition based on the Folio text or what they consider to be the most authoritative of the Quartos.

As this demonstrates, the texts we read or see performed are the results of editorial choices. This leads us to another important point: Shakespeare's *Hamlet* did not become a 'literary text' in his lifetime but over the course of centuries during which ambiguities surfaced, confirming the view that there can be no authoritative single original text. The history of *Hamlet* criticism, and that of the other tragedies, consists of numerous attempts to 'fix' the play's meaning. So in the discussions that follow, we will try not to 'fix' meanings in our consideration of how the four great tragedies work, but rather see how meanings are conferred on and flow from the texts as we read or experience them in a performance. We'll do this by considering not what the plays mean but how they work.

2

Hamlet (1600/1)

Rest, rest, perturbèd spirit!

(1.5.199)

As Chapter 1 showed, Shakespeare used structural formulae for his plays, and for tragedy he may have considered both a classical/neoclassical structure and perhaps a more relaxed one which allows for the complications of parallel sub-plots. In *Hamlet* the underlying five-part structure of the play allows for the interweaving of various sub-plots, with action in one plot prompting the growth of others throughout the play. We even find the structure allows for a play within a play, which reflects the story of the play and provides an opportunity for Hamlet to reflect on the nature of 'acting' and of dramaturgy. The classical concept of the three unities is nowhere observed in *Hamlet*. Shakespeare's play is about more than just the character who bears its name: the whole is as a mosaic of interactive designs of shade rather than just a linear narrative story. The elements considered in this chapter are merely indicative of the complexity of the work.

▶ Remembrance

Part of Shakespeare's craftsmanship is to make us believe in the action of the play while it is taking place, and we need to recognize how Shakespeare achieves this. In *Hamlet*, he exploits a world of memory. The play starts with talk of the past: a ghost is walking the battlements; the sentinels discuss the political situation caused by King Hamlet's slaying of King Fortinbras of Norway (1.1.89f.). The memory is political and has prompted a dangerous response, with young Fortinbras threatening to invade the Danes with a "Sharked up ... list of landless resolutes" (107). With the reappearance of the Ghost the two plots interweave from the first scene of the play. The next scene also starts with 'memory' as the new king, Claudius, reflects:

> *Though yet of Hamlet our dear brother's death*
> *The memory be green ...*
> *... we with wisest sorrow think on him*
> *Together with remembrance of ourselves.* (1.2.1–2, 6–7)

Reflection on the past, one in which Claudius has had a criminal hand, forces him to remember his own actions. Claudius has married the former king's widow, Gertrude, and usurped the throne, and now he wants to make his position secure. The issue of royal succession assuring political and social power and stability was a significant matter for Tudor England; the Reformation – prompted by Henry VIII's desire for a son to succeed him – was still recent history, and at the time of this play the last of Henry's heirs, the childless Elizabeth I, was in her late sixties.

The scene also reveals a further problem. Hamlet is locked in the past that the Ghost represents, and he continues to mourn his father's death, as exemplified by his mourning clothes: "But I have that within which passeth show;/These but the trappings and the suits of woe" (1.2.85–6). Shakespeare's evocation of a fictional memory takes us into the world of the play, and in particular into the inner life of the protagonist. The Ghost has a major dramatic function in emphasizing this, but also a thematic one. "Adieu, adieu, Hamlet: remember me" (1.5.96) are his parting words to Hamlet, but ironically, he implores his son: "Taint not thy mind nor let thy soul contrive/Against thy mother aught" (1.5.90–1). Hamlet's mind does get 'tainted' by the Ghost's story, even though we are never sure if his 'madness' is a protective cover; also, he almost contrives against his mother, though he says that he will "speak daggers to her" but not use them. Hamlet's reply to the Ghost is:

> *... Remember thee?*
> *Ay, thou poor ghost, while memory holds a seat*
> *In this distracted globe. Remember thee?*
> *Yea, from the table of my memory*
> *I'll wipe away all trivial fond records ...*
> *And thy commandment all alone shall live*
> *Within the book and volume of my brain*
> (1.5.100–4, 107–8)

So, remembrance drives the plot but also pulls the audience into the story, providing us with an external, fictional, historical narrative: events created by the dramatist that we are encouraged to think have happened before the actions of the play have begun. We take such techniques for granted because they are so well executed by Shakespeare. He manipulates the audience through using 'memory' as a point of reference throughout the play. Polonius, for example, is reminded by Hamlet that he once played on the stage (3.2.82f.), just as Hamlet has been reminded earlier that he had once heard the Player King recite a speech that "'twas caviar to the general" (2.2.383–4). Both examples may appear trivial but they keep up the suspension of our disbelief, compelling us to believe the story being told as history. At the same time Claudius works to erase memory, and it is this tension that contributes to the central 'action' of the play.

Other examples are more violent, as in the imagery of the first soliloquy when Hamlet speaks of his father's relationship with his Mother:

> *... Heaven and earth*
> *Must I remember? Why, she would hang on him*
> *As if increase of appetite had grown*
> *By what it fed on, and yet within a month –* (1.2.142–5)

The same 'memory' is taken up again in the confrontational chamber scene between Hamlet and Gertrude, as the prince forces her to look at the contrasting portraits of her dead husband and his successor:

> *Look here, upon this picture, and on this,*
> *The counterfeit presentment of two brothers.*
> *See what a grace was seated on his brow:*
> *Hyperion's curls, the front of Jove himself,* (3.4.60–3)

The gravedigger's scene comically playing on remembrances leads to Hamlet's "Alas, poor Yorick!" speech in which he contrasts the happiness of the past with the harsh, levelling reality of death (5.1.141f.). The exchange with the gravedigger prepares Hamlet for the much more serious matter of Ophelia's death, as the remembered 'antics' of the court jester give way to the more serious consequences of Ophelia's madness. Earlier, in her mad reverie, Ophelia had given out flowers to the court:

There's rosemary, that's for remembrance: pray, love, remember: and there is pansies, that's for thoughts. ... I would give you some violets, but they withered all when my father died. ... (4.4.180f.)

Violets were thought by the Elizabethans to be able to cure melancholy. They symbolized faithfulness and Viola (Italian for 'violet') was the name given by Shakespeare to the woman who is faithful in her love for Duke Orsino in *Twelfth Night*, a dark comic play written at about the same time as *Hamlet*.

Shakespeare's artistry is complex and hugely accomplished. Hamlet has put on a disposition of madness following the Ghost's revelation of the manner of his father's death, while Ophelia is portrayed as going mad due to her father's death. Her brother, Laertes, offers a third parallel in the way he deals with death. At the brief "obsequies" at Ophelia's grave, Shakespeare has Laertes recall those faithful violets, which, it is implied, could have cured Hamlet's melancholy:

Lay her i'th'earth:
And from her fair and unpolluted flesh
May violets spring! (5.1.188-90)

This is tightly controlled, highly skilled writing allowing us, the audience, to recall the withered violets that Ophelia gave to the queen. We are being taken into the fictional world through image, theme and remembrance; through, that is, the artistry of the dramatist.

▶ Morality and mortality

Some Liberal Humanist critics take as a starting point for discussion a Christian understanding of the relationship between morality and mortality. In such readings Shakespeare is credited with establishing an essential link between the tenets of Christianity and traditionally accepted concepts of universal truths. However, tragedy usually occurs at moments of doubt, and when distinctively human energies are shown to call metaphysical truth into question.

Eleanor Prosser, for example, considers the revenge-play tradition as capitalizing on an ethical dilemma produced within a Christian audience between what people believed about the divine operation of justice and what they felt when they saw its operations in the real world[12]. In other words, they felt an association, even an empathy, with the revenger undertaking revenge even though they believed that revenge itself was sinful. Such criticism is challenged by Cultural Materialists, who argue that to shift the focus from an overt theological reading to one which credits Shakespeare with the worldly wisdom of ethical manipulation is to remain within a form of critical perception that leads, as Drakakis puts it, to "the veneration of the dramatist"[13]. Drakakis, referring to Barthes, goes on to argue:

> Shakespeare as universal and eternal Man, and the body of the texts which he produced under determinate historical conditions as the repository

of human wisdom, function together to encourage both the eradication of the memory 'that they were once made' ... and to disguise the ideological process of reconstruction to which they are constantly subjected by the societies in which they now exist as manifestations of 'high culture'.[14]

This provides a challenge both for the Liberal Humanists and the Cultural Materialists in that within the context of any interpretation of the plays, Shakespeare's own ideology remains uncertain. There is an art in Shakespeare's detachment, but it is the detachment of uncertainty. He draws us in and pulls us away, offers us an orthodox viewpoint, but then presents alternatives to it. Where has the Ghost come from? If he is a figment of Hamlet's imagination, then Bernardo, Marcellus and Horatio are being drawn into the delusion. Shakespeare asks the question largely through the fictional construct of the protagonist. The whole premise of Hamlet's procrastination is one of questioning the meaning and purpose of life, of drawing to our attention particular issues so that we begin as an audience to make judgements of our own. These judgements are made from our perspective in the context of the performance's interpretation as a whole. We can look at the play as an historical document or – as we do when we see a performance – we can judge the various ways in which a production shapes the play in order to make it relevant to our current concerns. The play is a complex which cannot be reduced to a statement of a single ethical dilemma. A good dramatist is in tune with the issues of his age, and for us, a good performance is one that

▲ David Tennant (Hamlet) and Patrick Stewart (Claudius) in the 2008 RSC production.

allows us to make connections between a text from the past and our current preoccupations.

Historically Shakespeare is writing within a predominantly Christian culture which accepts a relationship between morality and mortality. The biblical story of Adam and Eve relates how eating the fruit of the tree of knowledge (traditionally associated with carnal knowledge) brings original sin into the world, while the Old Testament book of Leviticus forbids marriage to a brother's wife as incestuous. In *Hamlet*, Claudius has married his brother's wife, after first murdering the king as he slept in the garden. The Ghost reveals:

Ay, that incestuous, that adulterate beast,
... – won to his shameful lust
The will of my most seeming-virtuous queen. (1.5.47,
50–1)

This isn't quite the same circumstances as Henry
VIII, whose first wife (Catherine of Aragon) was the
widow of his dead brother Arthur, but Shakespeare is
in dangerous political territory nevertheless. It is a
territory, however, that he subsequently exploits with
the play within the play which is designed to "catch the
conscience of the King" (2.2.536–7). There is also here
the sense of 'seeming' rather than 'being', of putting on
an act rather than engaging in an 'action'. We may recall
Hamlet's earlier exchange with his mother "'Seems',
madam? Nay it is: I know not 'seems'." (1.2.76) and we
recall that he does not want to be judged by appearances
only. Claudius, in contrast, is nothing but appearances,
and for him the mask very rarely slips.

Like the Ghost, Hamlet regards the marriage as licentious,
and in Christianity, sin brought shame and death into the
world. Thus we have a constant flow of images through the
play about the flesh and its decay in death. In this context
Hamlet attacks not only Ophelia but women in general,
who "jig", "amble", "lisp", "nickname God's creatures"
and make "your wantonness your ignorance" (3.1.143–4).
This assault is misogynistic but also self-referential since
it is Hamlet the fictional dramatis persona who speaks
here. In his question "Why wouldst thou be a breeder of
sinners?" (3.1.125) is a disgust with himself at his own
sinful humanity, as someone "with more offences at my
beck [command] than I have thoughts to put them in,

imagination to give them shape, or time to act them in" (3.1.127–9). Shakespeare exposes the character as having a disgust with his selfhood, "What should such fellows as I do crawling between heaven and earth?"(3.1.129–30). This is all within an episode that has been preceded by the "To be, or not to be" soliloquy (3.1.62f.) with its contemplation of the act of suicide. In the face of the pains of the world, and despite the religious taboo on suicide as a mortal sin, Hamlet can contemplate it as "a consummation/Devoutly to be wished". (3.1.69–70). In the Latin Bible, Christ's last words are *Consummatum est* – "It is finished", or "It is accomplished". But this is not so for Shakespeare's Hamlet; neither his words here nor at his death give a sense of accomplishment. Elsinore may be a political reality rather than a Christian one, although when Hamlet confesses to Horatio that "there's a special providence in the fall of a sparrow ... the readiness is all" (5.2.150–2), Shakespeare may be implying that he has come to an acceptance of a divine plan that he cannot fully understand. What the fiction draws us into is the dilemma of how to 'act' when the very means whereby we explain action to ourselves, i.e. language, has become tainted. As we may reflect in the final scene, the language of the play itself cannot answer the question of whether what has happened is providential and moral or a series of accidents.

Mortality, similarly, permeates the imagery and the action of the play, with Yorick's skull being presented in the gravedigger's scene as an iconic metaphor for the transience of human life. This is an instantly recognizable visual image of great impact often used to characterize the play, appearing not only on play posters but on advertisements, stamps etc. It was created by the dramatist for a play written 400 years ago but probably only four years after the burial of his son (11 August 1596). "How long will a man lie i'th'earth ere he rot?", Hamlet asks the gravedigger (5.1.125). Shakespeare presents differing perceptions in the attitudes of his fictional characters to these issues, but he refrains from making judgements about the issues. This is, perhaps, why it is difficult to determine absolutely from the plays Shakespeare's own religious beliefs.

▶ Humanism

Critical opinion circles around humanism as a historical 'movement' and humanism as an 'ideology'. Humanism, like Christianity, promulgates the concept of a progressive history, which some contemporary criticism cannot accept. To Cultural Materialists, Shakespeare is of his time but not for all time. Within his time, he is necessarily interacting with the moral, ethical, and historical issues around him, one of which is a creative emphasis upon the centrality of 'Man' that comes under the heading of Renaissance humanism. In 1998 I published an article[15] which provides a fuller discussion on which I will now draw.

Paul Kristeller identifies four major concerns of what he terms the 'process' rather than the ideology of humanism. These are: a taste for elegance, style, neatness and literary form; the omnipresence of classical sources, quotations and ideas; an emphasis on man in his relationship with the universe; a tendency to express and consider worth expressing the concrete uniqueness of one's own opinions, experiences and surroundings[16].

A passage in the Second Quarto, but omitted from the First Folio, expresses in satiric vein the way in which courtiers affected a style of language and behaviour[17]. Osric is dressed as a courtier, with feathers in his hat similar to those that Rosencrantz and Guildenstern wore earlier in the play. He talks in an affected style and is ridiculed for it. He is modelled possibly on known characters but certainly on known characteristics. In 1561 the first English translation appeared of Castiglione's *The Book of the Courtier* (published 1528), a primer for the manners and conduct of the true courtier. In appearance and manner Osric is affecting to be a model servant of the court, inviting Hamlet to participate in a duel. In combat, Castiglione advises, the courtier "ought to worke the matter wisely in separating him selfe from the multitude, and undertake notable and bolde feates which hee hath to doe, with as little company as he can, and in the sight ... and especially in the presence and ... before the very eyes of his king"[18]. The duel in the play is about the planned murder of Hamlet but it is disguised under the affected courtiership of Osric. Shakespeare allows Hamlet to satirize Osric's behaviour, but also to reveal a perception beneath the foppishness or satire of the inevitability of death. There is one universal truth that certainly does exist since "the fall of a sparrow" is death. Nobody can deny that death will occur – "If it be now, 'tis not to come: if it be not to come, it will be now: if it be not now, yet it will come" (5.2.151–2) – but Shakespeare poses the question in a context that leaves the purpose of life and death uncertain. It is in the context of this uncertainty that the 'action' that we call tragedy is produced. At the point of his death Hamlet completes the Ghost's injunction, but the play leaves us in uncertainty as to whether the 'plot' is the work of "a special Providence" or of Hamlet's human ingenuity, or both, or is it a 'mystery'? To this extent, tragedy is a way of facing the inexorable fact of death.

Hamlet traverses a number of 'mysteries'. Earlier in the play the courtiers Rosencrantz and Guildenstern are taunted by Hamlet because they cannot play the recorder. Hamlet tears into them: "Why, do you think that I am easier to be played on than a pipe? Call me what instrument you will, though you can fret me, you cannot play upon me." (3.2.316–8). To have asked a courtier to play a recorder would have been an insult. Castiglione refers to instruments with frets as bringing about harmony[19]. Plutarch noted, however, that Alcibiades "refused to learn the flute, which he regarded as an ignoble accomplishment ... once a man starts blowing into a flute, his own friends can scarcely recognize his features"[20].

Shakespeare appears to be exposing the shallowness and affectation of the slight courtier in contrast to what Hamlet calls "the heart of my mystery" (3.2.313–4). Although Ophelia describes Hamlet as having been the perfect courtier:

O, what a noble mind is here o'erthrown!
The courtier's, soldier's, scholar's, eye, tongue, sword,
Th'expectancy and rose of the fair state,
The glass of fashion and the mould of form,
Th'observed of all observers, quite, quite down!
(3.1.147–52)

the protagonist delves beneath the tenets of Renaissance humanism as the play develops, undermining some of them with insult and satire as surely as he destroys the Danish court itself. He is portrayed simultaneously as being of the court and out of it, as a vehicle for providing a knowledge of humanism, and as a voice against it:

The time is out of joint: O, cursèd spite
That ever I was born to set it right! (1.5.205–6)

Shakespeare exposes contradictions in Hamlet the perfect Renaissance prince and through this the shallowness of courtly affectation and political hypocrisy. Humanism as an ideology was a historical reality for Shakespeare's time, manifested no doubt in fashionable behaviour at the court and elsewhere, even perhaps in the dress and behaviour of those in the sixpenny area of the theatre, dressed in their feathered hats. None of them could escape the play's bitter exposure, nor perhaps could the ideology itself. But Shakespeare merely questions, he does not answer.

For all the affectation of the courtiers at Elsinore, or the corruption of the court, the political threat is always hovering, as Act 4 Scene 3 helps to demonstrate. In the Folio the scene is very short but it does keep in our minds the pattern of the play and the fact that Fortinbras is never far away. Q2, however, provides an opportunity for a reflection on a war over "a little patch of ground/That hath in it no profit but the name" (lines 90–1) and for Hamlet to give the soliloquy "How all occasions do inform against me" (lines 105–39)[21]. It also establishes the nature of Fortinbras, whose polite message to Claudius – "If that his majesty would aught with us,/We shall express our duty in his eye" (4.3.5–6) – is a reminder to the Danish king, and to the audience, that 'I am still here, and the threat to your kingdom is not far away'. It helps to establish a sense of the warlike successor once Hamlet has completed his revenge. Throughout the play, profound questions are posed, but at the end of the play a leader emerges who resembles King Hamlet, and the narrative of what has happened becomes the responsibility of Horatio.

▶ Religious resonances

The speech "Not a whit, we defy augury: there's a special providence in the fall of a sparrow" (5.2.150–1) can be seen as a statement of the Calvinist concept of predestination. The concept can be paraphrased simply enough: if God is all knowing, then he knows from the time of your birth, indeed from all time, when you will die and whether you will go to heaven or hell; consequently your fate is predestined in that there is a limit to what you can do to influence your destiny. So Hamlet asserts, "There's a divinity that shapes our ends,/Rough-hew them how we will", an insight Shakespeare portrays him as having come to following the voyage towards England. To which Horatio responds, "That is most certain"(5.2.10–12). In Calvinism, God sustains Christians and "with singular providence" cares "for every one of those things that He hath created even to the least sparrow ... providence is called that, not wherewith God idly beholdeth from heaven what is done in the world, but wherewith as guiding the stern He setteth and ordereth all things that come to pass"[22].

Although Calvin accepted to an extent a concept of 'free will', Roman Catholicism laid a great emphasis upon it. Free will gives the individual choices for conduct but, more particularly, considers that God's grace can be bestowed upon the individual to protect and forgive sin even to the last breath. This would determine one's fate in the afterlife. Perfection, 'full grace', was the necessary condition for entry into heaven; imperfection of a gross kind (mortal sin) would sentence one to hell, while lesser imperfections (venial sin) would sentence one to Purgatory, where the sins would be purged to allow subsequent entry to heaven. Grace comes from the seven sacraments of the Church: baptism, confession, Eucharist (communion), confirmation, marriage, ordination, extreme unction (last anointing). *Hamlet* is strewn with the debris of Catholic sacramentalism as well as its religiosity but simultaneously it reflects Protestant ideas. It seems to dart from one doctrine to the other, exemplified maybe in the figure of a Catholic-inspired, purgatorial Ghost. David Scott Kastan points out that "Protestantism, we know, has no place for purgatorial ghosts ... The spirits of the dead do not return, and ghosts claiming otherwise are always a cheat."[23]

In Catholic terms, the Ghost comes from Purgatory since he complains that by his murder he was, "Cut off even in the blossoms of my sin,/ ... No reckoning made, but sent to my account/With all my imperfections on my head" and so cries out, "O horrible, O horrible, most horrible!" (1.5.81, 83–5). In his letter to the Hebrews in the New Testament, St Paul taught that forgiveness for sin comes only through the shedding of God's blood in the crucifixion of his son Jesus Christ. This shedding of the blood of Christ, who takes upon himself the burden of human sin, negates the necessity for human revenge. Shakespeare, clearly aware of these teachings, has his protagonist procrastinate by questioning the Ghost's injunction to 'revenge'. Moreover, he provides Claudius with a conscience, "O, my offence is rank, it smells to heaven" (3.3.39f.). It is a statement with a double effect. Claudius reveals to the audience that he is guilty of regicide and that, like the biblical Cain, he has murdered his brother. Claudius's hollow confession, in which he returns to type: "My words fly up, my thoughts remain below:/ Words without thoughts never to heaven go" (3.3.100–1) might, however, prompt the thought that Hamlet should have killed Claudius when he had the opportunity. By such reflections, Shakespeare pulls us into the dilemma that Hamlet faces, and prompts us to experience vicariously the impulse to compromise our moral principles and support the case for personal revenge.

The Ghost has not only been denied the sacrament of confession but has been murdered by an act that imitates the sacrament of extreme unction – anointing a dying person with holy oil on the five senses, including the ears. Claudius pours poison into his sleeping brother's ears and King Hamlet goes to the afterlife without atoning for his sins. An anointed or ordained king was thereby murdered, also debasing the sixth sacrament, that of consecrated or 'ordained' kingship.

Distortions of the sacraments appear throughout the play. In Catholicism a sacrament is an outward sign of inward grace. So what does the distortion signify? Ophelia, for example, is not cleansed by the water of baptism but drowns in water. Her death is proclaimed as being 'suspect' by the Church and she is not allowed to be buried in consecrated ground. At the end of the play, the wine in the communion cup, which in the sacrament of the Eucharist Catholics believe is transformed into the actual blood of Christ, is transformed into a deadly poisonous drink. It is intended for Hamlet but Gertrude drinks it in error, and it is later forced by Hamlet on Claudius. Similarly Claudius' earlier confession to God in his soliloquy (3.3.39f.) is frustrated. The confession does not bring the grace of forgiveness: since he is unable to repent, there can be no redemption (3.3.100–1).

Does this mean that Shakespeare was a Catholic or do the statements concerning predestination indicate him to be a Protestant? Such claims, in my view, are inappropriate to the literary critical questions to be asked of the text. What is shown is that Shakespeare was aware of the different sides of religious debate and used them for significant dramatic effect. The play draws on what we might call a residual Catholicism and an active Protestantism in a world where religious adherence had political consequences: in John Marston's play *The*

Malcontent, possibly written in the same year as *Hamlet*, the courtier Bilioso is asked "What religion will you be of now?" He pragmatically replies, "Of the duke's religion, when I know what it is."[24]

▶ Silence and last words

Shakespeare used the disputes and discussions of his time as another rich source to inform his plays, posing questions that are designed to get his audience thinking. Hamlet's last words, "The rest is silence" (5.2.307) are as ambiguous and enigmatic as the play itself. Is it that whatever is to follow cannot be told? Is it that now there is a 'rest', an ending of the burden of the dilemma in which he has been embroiled? Is it a Christian statement that silence or 'rest' follows the resolution of the 'action'? Or is it a more earthly and sceptical statement that after death there is nothing but silence? Is it a denial of an individuality constructed by a particular socio-political regime at Elsinore but that is now silent? Or is it simply, 'I'm dead. I'm silent'? There will be no ghost. 'Rest' in death is a Christian concept found in the prayer for the dead, "Eternal rest grant unto them, O Lord, and let perpetual light shine upon them". That is the release from Purgatory, the "rest" Hamlet is portrayed as wishing for the "perturbèd spirit" of his dead father. Perhaps it is implied by Shakespeare that it is the rest Hamlet would wish for himself. We can interpret this conclusion in many ways, although the play itself offers us something after Hamlet's 'silence', entrusted to Horatio who is enjoined by the dying prince to "Absent thee from felicity awhile,/And in this harsh world draw thy breath in pain,/To tell my story." (5.2.295–7), and then Fortinbras concludes the play.

These final words signal the drawing of the play to a close with the questions it has raised throughout still not fully answered; they are enigmatic, allowing us, like Horatio, to interpret the foregoing action. Horatio makes a judgement and provides a valuable perspective in the play:

> Now cracks a noble heart. Goodnight, sweet prince,
> And flights of angels sing thee to thy rest! (5.2.308–9)

Horatio appears to wish Hamlet a "rest" in heaven, as the words allude to one of the oldest prayers in Christendom, the *In Paradisum*, a prayer addressed not to God or to a saint but to the person who has died: "May angels lead thee to Paradise ... and bring thee into the holy city of Jerusalem. May the choir of angels receive thee and ... mayst thou have eternal rest."

We may conclude by observing that dramatists use the material they find to develop their plots, narrative, satirical perspectives, reflections. *Hamlet* does have a linear story, but as a play it is a mosaic of its time. We may impose our own meanings on it, we may enter into debate with it and we certainly reflect upon its questions. But we should not force meanings onto it because to do so would be to distort the play. In performance we try to understand how the play flows and at the same time try to identify its truths through our historical scholarship and criticism. Such is its richness, this is a play with which we can repeatedly engage and converse.

3

King Lear (1605/6)

Look, here comes a walking fire

(3.4.93)

Words are the opposite of silences. Words are made from breath, which is an indicator of life. Before words there is sound: "we came crying hither./Thou know'st the first time that we smell the air/We wail and cry" (*King Lear*, 4.5.177–9). Sound has to be heard, stimulating the senses which perceive the world and society around the living being, feeling, smelling, tasting, hearing, seeing. In *King Lear*, although Gloucester has been blinded, Lear tells him "Look with thine ears" (4.5.153–4). In Christianity, "the Word" is a metaphor of creation, of God the creator of all that is perceived, the breath of life, the final proof of existence, of the sense of being. Whether he was of Catholic or Protestant persuasion, Shakespeare was immersed in a Christian culture. In considering the religious culture and the theological disputation around him, David Scott Kastan sets aside speculation by affirming that all that can be meaningfully discussed is the way in which Shakespeare "recognized and responded to the various ways in which religion charged the world in which he lived"[25].

The dominant culture within which Shakespeare lived played a major role in helping to define the structure, plot and language of his plays. Within the story of Christ's life, there is birth, childhood, ministry, crucifixion and resurrection. It has been argued by critics, particularly O. B. Hardison, Jnr[26], that the great medieval mystery play cycles developed their structure from the Christian narrative that was central to the celebration of the Eucharist, a ritual that follows the pattern of Christ's life, death and resurrection. These mystery cycles and the parallel Christian morality plays of the medieval age came to an end with the Reformation in England and largely disappeared, although it is possible that as a boy Shakespeare may have seen some of them. The dramatists of the new Elizabethan age, however, created new structures of their own which questioned and challenged dominant cultural and social norms that depended on a desire for order, harmony and resolution, reflected in the narrative plots of the plays.

King Lear, widely regarded today as one of the most significant works of art in western culture, follows the structure found in Shakespearean tragedies: problems, journeys, arrivals, complications, silence. It emphasizes a more extreme version of Hamlet's "slings and arrows of outrageous fortune," (*Hamlet*, 3.1.64), boldly placing them on stage as an expression of experience. Once we begin to interpret the play through, for example, Aristotelian theories of audience reaction (*catharsis*) we start to move away from the play into something else, and we see how this led in the 18th century to a rewriting of the play and an adaptation of the plot .

Modern materialist criticism, as exemplified by Terry Eagleton, Malcolm Evans or Terence Hawkes, provides different radical perceptions of the play. John Drakakis notes that Eagleton's thesis is one whereby "*King Lear* generates a rhetoric which devalues language". It thereby "introduces a contradiction into the process of sign production whereby language is urged to surpass material reality at the same time as it is contained by it"[27]. In 'Letters on *King Lear*'[28], I argue that the play in performance is a complex system of communicative signs that amounts to a language in itself. I write: "Traditionally our empathy is with the tragic character of Lear but Lear is himself merely an element of language in a communication sign system that we call a play. He is a construct, a dramatically linguistic sign. He does not live. He in the context of his play communicates and signifies. In showing his breakdown of language Shakespeare affirms a faith in communicating with us"[29].

The play follows Shakespeare's fivefold structure, interweaving two parallel plots, the first concerning Lear and his daughters, the second Gloucester and his sons. They reflect each other like musical strains folding one theme upon the other, amplifying the dramatic effect of each story. The problems are announced in the opening scenes and the journeys, both mental and geographical, follow from them, with the two plots meeting in Act 4 Scene 5, when the blind Gloucester encounters the rejected and dejected king, who is moving in and out of madness:

Gloucester: *The trick of that voice I do well remember:*
Is't not the king?
Lear: *Ay, every inch a king.* (4.5.113–5)

This allows the two characters who suffer similar grief to compare their experiences, leading to a recognition scene for Lear, "Pray, do not mock me:/I am a very foolish fond old man", as he awakes to see "my child Cordelia" (4.6.62f.). But that recognition leads only to a further complication since events have been set in train that cannot be averted. Cordelia is later defeated and then hanged by Gloucester's illegitimate son, Edmund.

Gloucester, meanwhile, moves further into despair and it is left to his legitimate son, Edgar, disguised as Poor Tom, to comfort him:

Edgar: *What, in ill thoughts again? Men must endure*
Their going hence, even as their coming hither:
Ripeness is all: come on.
Gloucester: *And that's true too.* (5.2.10–13)

This comfort is ultimately to no avail and in Act 5 Scene 3 Edgar reports Gloucester's off-stage death.

Following the off-stage hanging in prison of Cordelia, the relation of words to breath is exposed in an extraordinarily powerful scene when Lear enters carrying the body of the dead Cordelia, crying out:

Howl, howl, howl! O, you are men of stones:
Had I your tongues and eyes, I'd use them so
That heaven's vault should crack. (5.3.264f.)[30]

Some editors assume that the 'howl' here is an instruction to the actor to articulate a response that is deeper than language can express. Even so, Lear reverts to the materials of language and the human senses. The reference is first to the tongue, the eyes, and then the hearing:

Cordelia, Cordelia! Stay a little. Ha?
What is't thou say'st? – Her voice was ever soft, (5.3.282–3)

Lear reflects she has "no breath at all?" and asks, "Pray you undo this button". Breath has gone and is going within him. Only sight remains as he looks at her and then, as the actor Robert Stephens did in 1993, beyond, into an abyss somewhere beyond the audience:

> *Do you see this? Look on her, look, her lips,*
> *Look there, look there!* (5.3.327–8)

So he breathes his last and dies. In the medieval morality play *Everyman*, the senses leave the central allegorical figure who represents humanity at the point of death. In *King Lear* they leave an individualized character, formed by the society which he once controlled as king but split rather than divided in what is a petulant power game about 'nothing'. For a modern audience, that 'nothing' has an existential force, but for an early Jacobean audience it echoed a biblical reference to unvarnished speech, of the kind that Cordelia champions.

▲ Warren Mitchell as King Lear in a 1995 production at the West Yorkshire Playhouse.

In *Shakespeare: Texts and Contexts*, Graham Martin and Stephen Regan consider the question of whether *King Lear* is a religious play, noting its pre-Christian imagery, but concluding that "Lear's world is not pre-Christian in such a way that its audience would think it entirely alien"[31]. Whereas *Hamlet* is haunted by the trappings of religion – heaven, hell, the ghost from purgatory, the emergence of Protestant individualism – and other references to residual Catholicism, God or any transcendent force shaping human destiny is largely absent from *King Lear*. There are many religious references, classical and Christian, but this play appears to focus, in one of its thematic areas at least, on differing perceptions or constructions of reality which conflict with one another to produce political and spiritual doubt. It is as if a large political canvas is downsized and domesticated so that the theatrical experience conveys a bleaker vision of existence than the end of *Hamlet*.

In each construction of a private reality by the major characters in the play, there appears to be a scepticism about all forms of order. But while we may speak of the characters of the play, modern productions of *King Lear,* with few exceptions, focus on the suffering of Lear and Gloucester. That suffering emanates from the decisions and actions of the characters themselves, although they are part of a panorama that we are invited to experience vicariously. This panorama proves to be greater than any of its parts, an issue which is raised and sustained throughout Grigori Kozintzev's film of *King Lear*, in which the actions of the king are shown to have serious social repercussions.

▶ Patterning: the comic and the tragic

Each of Shakespeare's four major tragedies has a distinctive identity. We may think of tragedy as a generic term embracing solemn plays of great emotional power that deal with characters of an elevated status who die in the end. But to reduce plays such as *King Lear* to the cosy definition of a single word 'tragedy' is to indulge in a grotesque and reductive shorthand. All Shakespeare's tragedies have their lighter – often very funny – moments, and our common perception of the term 'tragedy' can actually obscure their complex patterning and, with *King Lear*, the experimental power of the play, conveyed through linguistic and semiotic effects.

Many of the greatest productions of *King Lear* have circled around the problem implicit in its raw dialectic concerning nature, natural justice and the function of politics. Whether in Quarto or Folio, Shakespeare's original 'scripts' comprise a pattern or series of stark visual emblems: the king dividing his kingdom; Kent in the stocks; Edmund inflicting an injury on himself; Lear stripping himself naked on the barren heath; Gloucester's eyes being put out; Gloucester throwing himself from the top of a non-existent cliff; the old king entering with the body of his dead daughter.

These visual signs are linked to the language the characters deploy as they bewail, manipulate, prevaricate or court each other in a world of power, violence and lust; a world that in some respects is not dissimilar from our own. These epic moments bring to the fore a number of contradictions which are at the centre of the play, and are present in the two parallel plots.

As the play progresses, the questions seem to reflect Cordelia's stringently sparse response when Lear demands that she speak of her love for him. She says she has "nothing" to say. This is the first of a number of set pieces in the play which have real substance, but which at face value are 'nothing'. What is this challenge that Lear has set for Cordelia and his other daughters? Although Lear demands of his daughters:

> Which of you shall we say doth love us most,
> That we our largest bounty may extend
> Where nature doth with merit challenge? (1.1.42–4)

this episode is not a competition, since as soon as Goneril has spoken, the king gives her her land and as soon as Regan has spoken he gives her her land. This exchange is telling, however, in that Lear is asking his daughters to measure something, to render into crass sensory terms something that is immeasurable. You cannot quantify love, and in this staged competition we are invited to support Cordelia against her garrulous and, it turns out, deceitful sisters.

If it is not a competition, then what is this test about? It may be suggested that Shakespeare sees it as an indication of the way this fictional king imposes his authority: how does he perceive and construct reality here? Cordelia is going to get the best share because he believes that she will say that she loves him the most, and as his youngest daughter he expects her to look after him in his old age. Regan and Goneril will get their just share because they are his daughters. But behind this is a division of Lear's power-base, his land.

Shakespeare depicts Lear as having the power to construct not only his own reality, but reality per se. Because he has authority, everyone has to conform with the order, the ceremony, the games, the tests that he creates. But Cordelia will not conform; she is a woman who resists, her resistance attracting sympathy since Lear is clearly wrong in what he is doing. Like Hamlet, she "knows not seems". Her love "is" and so does not have to be proved; to do so would be to demean it. Lear is shown to be unable to understand.

In this respect, Lear is not dissimilar from another of Shakespeare's dramatic artefacts, Richard II, who at the beginning of *Richard II* (c.1595) relies on the great ceremonial order of the court. This order, however, is eventually frustrated by the more politically pragmatic strategies of his cousin, Bolingbroke, who refuses to be tied to these ceremonial laws. In *Richard II* the game is overtly political, but we also see the emotional toll it takes on the protagonist, as he comes to realize his dilemma at the moment when he has lost his power. *King Lear* is, up to a point, 'domestic'. But the king's 'family' extends to the entire community for which he has responsibility, so that everything he does is political.

Modern sensibilities may well agree with Cordelia's behaviour in that she refuses to be sycophantic. She tells the truth: that she will love her husband as a husband and her father as a father. Audiences old and new will recognize this as a familiar collective perception of reality, although this was an important issue of identity for women in the early 17th century. She doesn't perceive things very differently from what some would call 'common sense', but 'common sense' is itself a term that is ideologically loaded. For the 21st century this play is constantly one of challenge.

There is, however, something disturbing in Cordelia's response. Just as in *Richard II* the king cannot perceive that the unquestioning use of his authority will lead to revolt, so in his plan for retirement Lear cannot countenance any opposition to his monarchical power. In fact, Lear wants to separate the position of king from the responsibilities of kingship. Shakespeare has him warn Cordelia, "Nothing will come of nothing" and there is a certain truth in that. By not conforming to a ritual, Cordelia has put herself outside the order of things. It's not that nothing *will* come of nothing but that nothing *can* come of nothing because she refuses to be part of the material world that Lear constructs, in which everything is susceptible to measurement.

The further irony is that her revolt, together with his decision to abdicate, allow Goneril and Regan to pursue the logic of Lear's strategy to a horrifying conclusion:

Goneril: *Pray you let us sit together: if our father carry authority with such disposition as he bears, this last surrender of his will but offend us.*
Regan: *We shall further think of it.*
Goneril: *We must do something, and i' th'heat.* (1.1.306–10)

What they determine to create is a new domestic and political force into which the king, deprived of the symbols of his regal power, will have to fit. So it is that the play's patterns take shape. The argument about the 100 knights, for example, is a nonsense, but the logic is merely an extension of Lear's own logic. Within a very short space of time, Lear's 100 knights have been significantly reduced, and Kent, in the stocks, asks why Lear has so few followers about him. The Fool replies:

> *All that follow their noses are led by their eyes but blind men, and there's not a nose among twenty but can smell him that's stinking. Let go thy hold when a great wheel runs down a hill lest it break thy neck with following: but the great one that goes upward, let him draw thee after. When a wise man gives thee better counsel, give me mine again:*
> (2.2.244–8)

Thus the argument that follows between Lear and Regan and Goneril turns Lear's logic against him, and aims to reduce him to 'nothing'.

▶ The heath

What, the play might ask, is the foundation of any reality, any perceived truth? Edgar and Gloucester in the parallel plot are tricked into believing a story which is fictitious, Edmund's deceitful narrative. The result is that Edgar is forced to flee and he takes on the persona of 'Poor Tom' out on the heath. Many productions of the play, and many criticisms of the play, seem to view Poor Tom as some kind of Elizabethan John the Baptist, sent out in a loin cloth to eat insects and wild honey in the wilderness. He wails and moans until he leads Gloucester to the "Ripeness is all" statement (5.2.12). In fact, he becomes the emblem of the 'unaccommodated man' of whom Lear has, up to this point in the play, taken no account.

To portray a quaint Tom, flimsily dressed and crying out in a squeaky voice that "Tom's a cold" is, to my mind, a misleading rendering of the role. We have to consider what he is actually saying. Tom is "cold" because exposure to the cold is the only reality that Tom knows. All other measures of reality, including his name, have been usurped by lies masquerading as truths. Edgar's own perception of social order has disappeared; it has been stolen by his illegitimate brother, who is aware that the currency of power is land. But the heath to which those who have been displaced resort is a wasteland, barren, worthless, open to the ravages of the elements. Edgar isn't on the heath just to lead Gloucester. He is there as an emblematic figure, reconstructing an identity that has been taken from him. He has had to begin again and with a new name in order to find himself again. This echoes the plight of the usurped Richard II: "I have no name, no title;/No, not that name was given me at the font,/But 'tis usurped" (*Richard II*, 4.1.250–2).

It seems that Shakespeare, in a complex pattern of interactive elements, is examining aspects of identity, experience and perception in order to pose questions about the whole nature of reality. The very opening of the play offers us some indication; the awful puns Gloucester makes about Edmund's conception are not just for comic effect. Gloucester may laugh and joke about Edmund's bastardy but Edmund shows in his Act 1 soliloquy that he can turn his illegitimacy to his political advantage, and he does so by appealing to the unmediated biological truths of 'Nature' (1.2.1–22). Edmund transforms Gloucester's jokes into a new alternative reality, and he does so by engineering a shift of emphasis in the very foundations of domestic society, so that his brother Edgar becomes the victim rather than the legitimate heir. He can do this because Shakespeare depicts him as realizing that society's rules are not hard and fast, that there is a gap between the values and attitudes prescribed by law and actual human behaviour, and that this gap can be exploited.

It is not so much poor Tom as victimized Tom, who Shakespeare depicts as having to suppress his bitterness to combat the turning of the ideological tide. On the heath he becomes the victim of the 'cruelty' of nature, subject to the wind, rain and tempest, with only a hovel to accommodate or protect him. But he creates a strong enough identity for himself at the end of the narrative to be able to defeat Edmund and regain his birthright.

What is the devil that Edgar describes (4.5.82–5), claiming he sees at the top of the cliff a devil that has led Gloucester to contemplate suicide. Some might argue that it is something Edgar uses to help educate his father, although we should bear in mind that Edgar uses an allegorical cloak to protect himself in what is a hostile environment. Gloucester himself is also a victim of that hostility but after he throws himself from the imaginary cliff, he does not know whether he is alive or dead, whether he has fallen or not. In the play, the disguised Edgar claims to provide a particular experience for his disillusioned and blind father, and he does so from a position in which he is himself marginalized from his society. The play asks a series of questions: Who are you when you have been rejected, stripped of your power and social status or sent out on to the heath blinded or robbed of your birthright? Moreover, the play seems to offer a perverted view of Christianity in that the secularized Lear, realizing his own potentially tragic situation and fearing his own sanity, calls not on a god or a religious figure in his anguish but on his Fool:

> ... But this heart shall break into a hundred thousand flaws,
> Or ere I'll weep. O fool, I shall go mad! (2.2.473–4)

Belief offers no consolation for the pain and the madness that Lear suffers and which will eventually result in his death. In an incisive exchange with the Fool at the end of the first Act, Lear similarly prays:

> O, let me not be mad, not mad, sweet heaven!
> Keep me in temper: I would not be mad! (1.5.34–5)

In Jonathan Miller's production of the play, he had an old Lear and an old Fool come face to face in the expression of such anxiety. All of this may have what is traditionally seen as a tragic effect but there is something mingled with it that is more challenging than the Aristotelian notion of *anagnorisis* or self-recognition will allow. A blind man throwing himself from a non-existent cliff is farcical and it contributes to a sense of the ludicrous fragility of a reality that no longer encourages belief.

Each event, and each character, is part of a dramatic discourse at the heart of which there appears to be nothing except illusion and disorder, an irrationality that informs human conduct. Lear appears to conform to a familiar definition of absurdity: abdicating, forced onto an inclement heath, taking off his clothes in a storm, trying to find out who he is. The clothes are the trappings of the society he is responsible for having created, and yet, as he comes to realize in his encounter with Poor Tom, 'unaccommodated man' is something that he has failed to consider. On the heath he has to become as Poor Tom. He has to find out who he is now that language, ceremony and order have broken down. Everything is stripped away. He has to stand naked, exposed to the elements. Shakespeare takes King Lear beyond the realms of civilized communication to a point where he addresses Nature – the wind, rain and cold – rather than society:

> Blow winds and crack your cheeks! Rage, blow,
> You cataracts and hurricanoes, spout
> Till you have drenched our steeples, drown the cocks!
> You sulphurous and thought-executing fires,
> Vaunt-couriers of oak-cleaving thunderbolts,
> Singe my white head! And thou, all-shaking thunder,
> Strike flat the thick rotundity o'th'world!
> Crack nature's moulds, all germens spill at once
> That makes ingrateful man! (3.2.1–9)

In the 21st century we sit and reverently witness the tragic farce of this man reduced to nakedness and at the mercy of a violent storm. If he takes off everything, as did G. Wilson Knight in the 1930s and Ian McKellen in 2007, we can become distracted by the nakedness. In a modern production, complete nakedness (which may not have occurred on the Elizabethan or Jacobean stage) is difficult to interpret symbolically, although that is what the play asks us to do. What audiences are being asked to witness is the breakdown of the stability of the self and the social context that sustains it. In the end, the body is primarily natural, not social, and therefore once rejected by society, divorced from an identity within society, all that remains as a yardstick for judgement is Nature, the body outside the institutions of society, the body that will die and decompose, the naked body that on the scaffolds and gibbets of Elizabethan and Jacobean England was castrated, disembowelled and quartered, and its separated parts sent to the far reaches of the land so that at the Last Judgement it could not be reunited for final redemption.

This vision is central to the confrontational nature of this play. Shakespeare is challenging social perceptions of reality. If Lear constructs a reality that ultimately collapses, so do Regan and Goneril, so do Gloucester and Edmund, and so, in a curious way, does Cordelia. This is a domestic affair but at the same time it is not a family affair. In this conceptual framework, 'vice' or 'virtue' per se have little to do with the issue. Each character is frustrated, more or less, in their individual attempts to resolve satisfactorily the problems that they encounter. It is not a thesis and antithesis leading to synthesis; it is rather a raw expression of the agony of what it can mean to be human in an inward, self-harming society driven by vicious ambition and cruelty.

At the end of the play Edgar feels all he can do is be pragmatic and obey the demands of time:

The weight of this sad time we must obey:
Speak what we feel, not what we ought to say. (5.3.344–5)

It is precisely this conflict between what is felt and what ought to be done that cannot be resolved, largely because there is a gulf between signification (the capacity of language to express a stable reality) and reality itself.

Out on the heath as Gloucester approaches king, madman, fool and retainer, the Fool cries "Look, here comes a walking fire" (3.4.93). He describes what his senses perceive. It is the Fool who keeps saying 'let's go in, it's too wet to be outside'. It's the madman, Poor Tom, who keeps complaining of the cold. We are offered here a bleak vision of society, stripped of the sophistications of social living, and in the end signifying nothing. This is a state of mind to which Shakespeare also leads Macbeth (*Macbeth*, 5.5.28).

In *King Lear*, the untying of the knot is the process of the play, as found in the neoclassical definition of tragedy. Our classification of this as a 'tragedy' is one way of explaining what in another context is seen as the cruel joke played upon man by 'the gods'. Gloucester says:

As flies to wanton boys are we to th'gods:
They kill us for their sport. (4.1.41–2)

This is Gloucester's way of accounting for what happens to him, and it is this that Edmund refutes absolutely in his first soliloquy of the play. The 'gods' in this case are remote and inaccessible; they are, more importantly, a delusional refuge, a solace, an escape. To the end the play portrays absurdity, vacuity, nothingness, the chaos upon which we seek to impose order. That is not to say that the play negates the necessity of creating these myths. On the contrary, it demands that in recognizing that we construct ways of seeing and ordering the world, we understand the human condition and predicament from beginning to end. Lear in his madness recognizes Gloucester and emphasizes his name, the identifier of the person before him, just as Gloucester acknowledges Lear's 'natural' demeanour as a king. But Lear does not stop there; he moves on to the naked experience of birth as part of the cycle of existence: "thy name is Gloucester./Thou must be patient; we came crying hither." (4.5.176–7)

Naming is the first step in the social construction of reality after birth. At the end of the play, Lear is depicted as dying. He does not live on, as the 18th century wished him to do. But it is art that transcends time by communicating experience from one historical epoch to the next. In drama, the illusion is the play itself. And it is in the mobilization of the elements of the play that we find the dramatist's optimism. Despite its depiction of horrors, the play affirms a belief in trans-historical humanity that the audience can recognize. In the play itself we recognize both tears and laughter, and possibly a questioning hope for a future that might be able to avoid these pitfalls.

For the 21st century, Shakespeare's drama has become a part of the social order but if we compartmentalize his writings too neatly, too cosily, they will lose their significance. They will become subject to what some would regard as a vacuous neo-conservative liberal humanism that is very different from the humanism to which Shakespeare was exposed. Shakespeare then will have fallen victim to Lear's condition: thoughtless and irresponsible shortsighted politics will have become the reality.

If, on the other hand, we acknowledge the confrontational nature and demands of *King Lear* as tragedy, and as comedy, and register its engagement with absurdity, then the drama's significance may be found in the wisdom and the simple perception of the Fool:

> *Prithee, nuncle, be contented: 'tis a naughty night to swim in. Now a little fire in a wild field were like an old lecher's heart, a small spark, all the rest on's body cold. Look, here comes a walking fire.* (3.4.91–3).

It is, perhaps, in his expressed experience of nature and the political constructed environment in which he exists that we can see why Shakespeare's *King Lear* matters.

4

Macbeth (1606?)

So foul and fair a day
I have not seen

(1.3.39)

Great actors have the awesome ability to make audiences believe in fictional characters as if they were real people. As preceding chapters have illustrated, Shakespearean texts show how audiences can be manipulated so that they are taken into the illusion of the drama. During the course of a play, the actors can promote a suspension of disbelief, making the audience forget that they are watching a play.

But Hamlet, Othello, King Lear and Macbeth are fictional constructs and have no existence outside the dramatic events in which they are involved onstage. So for a critic to ask, for example, questions about the events leading up to the marriage of Gertrude and Claudius, their fictional courtship or their deception of Old King Hamlet is to fall into the trap of working from within the suspension of disbelief to provide the dramatic characters with extra-theatrical lives, lives that resemble the everyday experience of the audience. We are right, however, to ask why Shakespeare tells us that Hamlet was educated at Wittenberg, the city where Martin Luther made the famous protest that led to the rise of Protestantism. This question may be pertinent to the protagonist's function in the play, since it tells us something about the motive for Hamlet's persistent and profound doubt as he encounters the world of Elsinore. In this context we can appreciate the irony of L. C. Knights' famous essay, 'How Many Children had Lady Macbeth?'[32]. In the title itself L. C. Knights challenges a school of criticism whose attention to detail had become diverted by realism and characterization from the concerns of the play itself. Knights refers to a detail in

Shakespeare's play where the apparently childless Lady Macbeth claims, in passing, that she has "given suck" [breastfed] to an infant (1.7.58), even though Macduff states (at 4.3.249) that Macbeth has no children. For the critic it is fallacious to explain what appears to be a narrative inconsistency with such questions. To encourage debates about whether Lady Macbeth had borne a child by another man or whether the child she had 'suckled' had subsequently died, for example, is to be diverted from the events of the play. But to acknowledge the inconsistency and to ask why it is there can lead us down a more productive avenue of enquiry.

One answer may be that what matters is the immediate emotional effect produced by these revelations. It is important to recognize Lady Macbeth's inhumanity at the moment she disowns the natural responsibilities of motherhood; unlike Macbeth himself, she cannot dispense "the milk of human kindness" exemplified in the suckling of an infant and the nurturing of life. The characters, the narrative, the poetry, the accompanying emotional effects, the themes, the action, the set, the theatre of the performance, even the narrative inconsistencies and apparent contradictions, are all part of the communicative process of the drama.

Instead of following A. C. Bradley's literary critical method, L. C. Knights promoted an alternative critical approach, but one that had its roots in the early 19th-century Romantic emphasis on the language of the play: the finer the language, the finer the play. Knights takes A. C. Bradley to task for claims that Macbeth was 'exceedingly ambitious', that he must have been so by temperament and that the tendency must have been greatly strengthened by his (Macbeth's) marriage. Knights also regards as irrelevant to the drama "conjecture upon Hamlet's whereabouts at the time of his father's death"[33]. This leads him to ask how we should read Shakespeare. He proposes: "That more complete, more intimate possession can only be obtained by treating Shakespeare primarily as a poet" and he continues to explain that by reading the play as a dramatic poem we "elucidate the meaning ... unravel ambiguities", by estimating "the kind and quality of the imagery". This determines "the precise degree of evocation of particular figures", allowing "full weight to each word", exploring its 'tentacular roots' and discovering "how it controls and is controlled by the rhythmic movement of the passage". He concludes, "In short, we have to decide exactly why the lines 'are so and not otherwise'"[34].

Other critics, particularly H. Granville-Barker and G. Wilson Knight, looked towards the performance elements of the dramas, and to their origins as plays, not realistic novels. Wilson Knight, quoted by Knights, regards *Macbeth* as exemplifying an all-embracing evil, seeing characters as "not human at all, but purely symbols of a poetic vision"[35], while L. C. Knights regarded the play as "a statement of evil; but it is a statement not of a philosophy but of ordered emotion"[36].

Similarly Jan Kott's remarks on the play, although possibly not quite as pertinent as when he wrote them in 1960s, have a general appeal that can be adapted to fit any 'contemporary' event:

History in Macbeth *is confused the way nightmares are; and, as in a nightmare, everyone is enveloped by it. Once the mechanism has been put in motion, one is apt to be crushed by it ... History in* Macbeth *is sticky and thick like a brew or blood.*[37]

Kott's perspective revealed his contemporary experience but this leads us in considering this play into a problematic area. Kott speaks of 'history' but how is history defined? How is 'history' read, not just in the theatre but in education? It is too easy to reduce this play to a polarized opposition between good and evil. We might ask whether this was true of the play at the time of its inception? What were the social and political influences prevalent at the time of its writing, and how does this knowledge affect our contemporary readings? The Cultural Materialist challenge in this regard has been to the historical depiction of a stable world-view propounded by the critic E. M. W. Tillyard[38]. Such a world-view, of a stable belief and a sense of the universal truth that accompanies it, was thought to manifest itself through an ordered 'chain of being', although with hindsight this has more to do with ideology than historical fact, an ideology to which critics such as E. M. W. Tillyard appear to have been sympathetic.

▶ Readings of the play

Since his plays were first produced a relationship has been built up between the dominant ideology of a Protestant Christian culture and Shakespearean texts.

Critics have questioned such common beliefs about Shakespeare. E. A. J. Honigmann in *Shakespeare: The 'Lost Years'*[39] draws together a number of 'coincidences' found in a variety of historical texts, together with certain anecdotal evidence, to raise the questions of a Catholic influence on Shakespeare. Honigmann's study suggests that Shakespeare may have been a teacher, working for two Roman Catholic families in Lancashire. Other biographies of Shakespeare have pointed towards the probable recusant Catholicism of his father as well as that of a teacher, John Cottam, at the grammar school in Stratford-upon-Avon where it is thought that Shakespeare was educated. The 'coincidences' build up in Honigmann's study to point towards the possibility of Shakespeare having Roman Catholic sympathies. How does this relate to *Macbeth*? The play was probably written in 1606, the year following the Gunpowder Plot, in which Roman Catholics had attempted to blow up James I and the Houses of Parliament, but the play is also sometimes read as a political allegory of issues that are of relevance to the Reformation.

David Scott Kastan, however, sounds a warning about taking religious interpretations of the plays to the point where they produce "readings that seem to prove only that any text can be allegorized rather than that these texts should be"[40]. He questions criticism which focuses on *Macbeth* as a "figurative history of the English Reformation" in which parallels are drawn between the fictional Scottish king and queen of Shakespeare's play and the historical figures of Henry VIII or Elizabeth I. Such allegorical readings go beyond the language of the play. If, in our reading or interpretations of these plays, we generate our own meanings from reading or seeing a Shakespeare play, we still cannot entirely divorce Shakespeare from that process. So we cannot impose arbitrary, unreliable, idiosyncratic or even anarchic interpretations on the work.

If actors, audiences and readers are part of a conversation with the texts, then, as with all meaningful conversations and debate, there has to be an element of balance or respect accorded to what is being said. In theatrical production and criticism there has to be an integrity that informs interpretation. In the case of *Macbeth*, the play was written at a time of much controversy and treason involving Roman Catholicism. Religion cannot, therefore, be far away from any discussion of the play, but nor can the fact that a Scottish king had recently ascended the throne of England, and that a significant political change had taken place with the change from the Tudor to the Stuart dynasty. At this period monarchical power was absolute and thus it invited flattery. It may be that *Macbeth* was intended to flatter the new king, although Shakespeare's method seems to have been much more subtle than the term 'flattery' suggests.

How does this affect our reading of *Macbeth*? It questions the encapsulation of 'history' into categories, and particularly into an 'Elizabethan world-view' category. Some contemporary criticism challenges the readings of Liberal Humanist critics that start from the position of a particular established universal 'truth' through history. So Alan Sinfield, writing in 1992 on *Macbeth*, began to ask questions that challenged orthodox interpretations.

For example, he points to the fact that Macbeth, in killing the rebel Macdonald, is hailed as a great warrior by King Duncan, who calls him a "valiant cousin" and a "worthy gentleman", but when Macbeth kills King Duncan he is subsequently seen as a murderer. Sinfield writes: "Violence is good ... when it is in the service of the prevailing dispositions of power; when it disrupts them, it is evil" and he argues that "Macbeth focuses major strategies by which the state asserted its claim"[41]. Sinfield concludes that although certainly portrayed as "a murderer and an oppressive ruler", the character is in effect "one version of the absolute ruler, not the polar opposite"[42]. Such readings in the context of changing ideologies, notions of historical accuracy or universal truth, prompt the modern critic to challenge and review what has been hitherto regarded as critical orthodoxy. *Macbeth* in the past may sometimes have been seen as an easier play to study than the other three great tragedies, but today it still has relevance to certain questions, particularly those concerning the definition of 'good' or 'evil' as determined by society.

▶ Equivocation and treachery

The Gunpowder Plot was not the first attempt on the new king's life. In 1600 the Scottish Earl of Gowrie had attempted to assassinate James while the king was Gowrie's guest. Thus there was a real-life parallel to the assassination by Macbeth of the king who was lodging under his protection. In *Macbeth* there appear to be a number of references and compliments to James I. It has been suggested that the play was performed at court in 1606 when the king was entertaining the king of Denmark. In *Macbeth, Text and Performance*, Gordon Williams refers to the many allusions throughout the play to the Gunpowder assassination attempt. He demonstrates how a conventional reading of Act 4 Scene 1, where the weird sisters show Macbeth the vision of the eight kings, would have produced a spectacle of extraordinary power on stage if, as is believed, it was presented before James I and the Danish king. The scene, according to Williams, would have shown: "the genuine amity and perfect safety accorded this royal guest in contradistinction to the treatment meted out to Duncan"[43]. Williams notes in particular the traditional theory that the actor playing Banquo may have pointed to James I during the play at Whitehall Palace as kings of Scotland of Banquo's lineage are shown by the witches to Macbeth. Such is an acceptable, traditional speculation on a scene which portrays a number of the kings holding familiar political emblems linking them closely to James, "some I see/That two-fold balls and treble sceptres carry" (4.1.129–30). The idea that James I was of Banquo's lineage is found in Shakespeare's main source for the play, Holinshed's *Chronicles*, but was first recorded, as Williams notes, by the "propagandist-historian, Hector Boece"[44], some of the details from whose *History of Scotland* appear in Shakespeare's play but not in Holinshed. The image of the "two-fold balls" refers to the monarchies of England and Scotland, united for the first time by the accession of James I in 1603.

This show takes place in a nightmare vision being presented to Macbeth, who sees it as a "Horrible sight!" (4.1.131). We might speculate that if Shakespeare was a Catholic sympathizer, then the collocation of the words "Horrible sight" with the image of the twin balls and triple sceptre denoting the reign of James I may perhaps have sounded a note of artistic humour or satire on the dramatist's part. Artists are sometimes known to play such dangerous games.

Similarly, the murder of a Scottish king as a central motif of the play can be read in two ways. The first is in accordance with a traditional literary orthodoxy, but the second would see the regicide as a potentially subversive, dramatic event that issued a challenge to the philosophy of the 'divine right' of kings that James I was known to support. This was the philosophy to which Claudius had appealed in *Hamlet* when confronted by the rebellious Laertes: "There's such divinity doth hedge a king/That treason can but peep to what it would,/Acts little of his will" (*Hamlet*, 4.4.123–5).

The play in this regard appears to be equivocal. James I was a voyeur who used his power over his courtiers for his own sexual gratification. Duncan is portrayed often as a holy man (as, for example, by Griffith Jones in the 1976 RSC production), but another reading might suggest that he is the man who sends his thanes off to war while he looks on. Duncan says, "There's no art/To find the mind's construction in the face" (1.4.13–14), implying the equivocation and hypocrisy which permeates the play. Under both the Tudors and the Stuarts, Catholic sympathizers, seen as traitors, were publicly hanged, disembowelled while still alive and quartered at Tyburn (near to where Marble Arch now stands). Such was the fate of the Jesuit priest Henry Garnet, for his supposed complicity in the Gunpowder Plot, in the spring of 1606. One of the 'main crimes' levelled at the Jesuits (members of the Society of Jesus, a Roman Catholic order of priests) was that of equivocation, of saying one thing to disguise another, potentially more incriminating meaning. Indeed, at his trial, Garnet had attempted to justify the practice and Shakespeare alludes to Garnet as one of those entering the hell's gate of Macbeth's castle in the Porter's scene:

Faith, here's an equivocator that could swear in both the scales against either scale, who committed treason enough for God's sake, yet could not equivocate to heaven: O, come in, equivocator. (2.3.6–9)

The theme of 'equivocation' is central to the play, and at the end Macbeth himself comes to "doubt th'equivocation of the fiend/That lies like truth" (5.5.46–7). Indeed, with the weird sisters' "Fair is foul and foul is fair", what we might regard as the normal referential properties of language are inverted so that meanings are the opposite of what we might expect. In this way Macbeth encounters a Birnam Wood that is not Birnam Wood, and he finally dies at the hand of an adversary who was not, albeit only in a technical sense, "of woman born".

▶ Temptation and consequences

Macbeth is a bloody play, charged with sexual power to the point of being animalistic in its barbarity. What Lady Macbeth says about ripping the suckling child from her breast and dashing its brains out (1.7.58–63) in her determination that her husband should secure power through murder is a very powerful image of the destruction of innocence. It is, possibly, the ultimate crime: the mother killing her child. It could equate to the subject killing the monarch but goes beyond it, since monarchs by their own actions lose their innocence, but babies cannot. So maybe we have here a different reading of the image itself in the overall narrative context of the play. This is the power of the Shakespearean text, the rich ambiguity at its heart which invites a variety of response.

Macbeth is given a conscience, which emerges in the illusions he sees – the dagger before him (2.1.40ff.), the ghost of Banquo (3.4.52ff.) – and, throughout the play, an inevitability about his curiosity in an underworld where he cannot tell whether the phantoms before him, the weird sisters, are male or female, and whether they speak the truth or not. Is what they are saying true or false? Ironically it is both, as they prove their credibility in pointing to or helping determine the future to the very end. Because of their grotesque appearance, the strange rituals in which they engage and their grotesque pot of broth, the audience is exposed to a palpable form of evil. All that the weird sisters predict actually happens but does what they say make it happen? To ask that question is to demonstrate that Shakespeare has drawn us into the play. It is the dramatist who makes the play happen; his dramatic characters are vehicles that carry the action forward to its conclusion. Macbeth in the soliloquy at 1.3.140f. balances probabilities against realities, imaginings against conclusions with the equivocal tautology, "And nothing is, but what is not" (line 152). In this way Macbeth draws attention to the process of equivocation as well as to the temptation that it seems to offer him. The Christian man is being drawn to heinous sin, to the thing that he desires, but along with the desire comes a consideration of its consequences – a 'conscience', in other words – that recognizes the sinfulness of the temptation even as Macbeth succumbs to its attractions. He is a more intense version of Claudius's more perfunctory stirrings of conscience in *Hamlet*:

> *...Present fears*
> *Are less than horrible imaginings:*
> *My thought, whose murder yet is but fantastical,*
> *Shakes so my single state of man*
> *That function is smothered in surmise,*
> *And nothing is, but what is not.* (1.3.147–52)

Shakespeare has Macbeth say in the same speech that the "horrid image" of the deed he is imagining does "unfix my hair". The portrayal is of an enthusiasm and an excitement for what, at this stage, is nothing more than a fantasy encapsulating a desire to do the almost unthinkable, by living what is imagined. It is a strange voyeurism of one's own thoughts, a submission to what Christianity terms 'temptation'. Dramatically, these temptations are spurred on by the embodiment of the weird sisters' evil. Yet the consequences that occur are not postponed to the afterlife but follow immediately on from the deed itself.

The soliloquy "Is this a dagger which I see before me ... A dagger of the mind, a false creation,/Proceeding from the heat-oppressèd brain?"(2.1.40, 45–6) appears similarly to be the product of temptation, a pre-vision of the deed and its danger but also a luxuriating in it, an enjoyment of its process. These reflections are not specifically about right or wrong but about the process of a deed that in the context of the play is clearly wrong. Even Macbeth's statement to his wife that "We will proceed no further in this business" (1.7.32) can be interpreted as a request for further confirmation of the resolution to realize in action a dangerous fantasy. Lady Macbeth's "unsex me here" speech (1.5.34–52) must rank as one of Shakespeare's greatest achievements. In her determination to be "unsexed", Lady Macbeth deploys a powerful sexual imagery that aligns, but in a sado-masochistic manner, sexual union with personal gratification. The negative wish invoked the positive enjoyment of the self-cursing: "Make thick my blood,/Stop up th'access and passage to remorse" (41–2); "Come to my woman's breasts/And take my milk for gall" (45–6); "Come, thick night,/And pall thee in the dunnest smoke of hell" (48–9). This is a sexual union with the darkness of death itself and at the end of the speech Shakespeare depicts Lady Macbeth as changing sex in crying that her phallic "keen knife see not the wound it makes,/Nor heaven peep through the blanket of the dark,/To cry 'Hold, Hold!'" (50–2). Here under the "blanket" of the night, as in a bed, is the sexual climax of the deed: the spirits that she invokes at the start of the speech all point to her enjoyment of the act. It is a speech of impressive sexual power exposing a disturbed imagination. Lady Macbeth has become one with the darkness that accompanies her desire, and it is a path that Macbeth himself will shortly follow.

▲ Elliot Cowan (Macbeth) and Laura Rogers (Lady Macbeth) in a 2010 production at the Shakespeare's Globe Theatre.

With the deed done, and the hands of both Macbeth and Lady Macbeth physically covered in blood (2.2.75), Shakespeare starts to move us from the world of temptation and diseased imagination into the world of consequences. Macbeth deludes himself that he has the power to see "the future in the instant", and that he can therefore control events. However, even though in the stages leading up to the regicide he is fully aware of the moral implications of the act, in the wake of the deed itself he becomes paranoid as the future begins to slip away from him; believing in the accuracy of the weird sisters' prediction that it is Banquo's lineage that will succeed to the throne of Scotland, Macbeth muses that "To be thus is nothing, but to be safely thus" (3.1.51). To secure his own future, he must kill Banquo, but no matter what he does, there is always something – in this case, Banquo's son Fleance – that escapes his grasp.

The fantastical imaginings of the aspiring protagonist and his ambitious spouse, once converted into actions, return to torment the perpetrators. The rich and vivid imagery of the play invites us to experience vicariously the act of murder: Macbeth hears a voice crying, "'Sleep no more,/Macbeth does murder sleep'" (2.2.42–3), and later Lady Macbeth is seen sleepwalking, described by the Doctor as "A great perturbation in nature, to receive at once the benefit of sleep and do the effects of watching" (5.1.7–8). In washing her hands in her sleep, "Out, damned spot! Out, I say!" (5.1.26), she contradicts her statement following the murder, when she claimed "A little water clears us of this deed" (2.2.78). On the whole, the horrifying consequences of their deeds far exceed even the imaginations of the protagonist and his wife, to the point where, as Lady Macbeth laments, they unwittingly sacrifice their 'content': "Naught's had, all's spent,/Where our desire is got without content" (3.2.6–7).

Macbeth's earlier question "Will all great Neptune's ocean wash this blood/Clean from my hand?" (2.2.71–2) is answered through the process of the play in the negative. Textually it might remind us of another play, and another context. In *Richard II* (1595/6) the king tells his followers: "Not all the water in the rough rude sea/ Can wash the balm from an anointed king" (*Richard II*, 3.2.49–50) and in the same speech draws a comparison between darkness and light, when the sun rises, "And darts his lightning through ev'ry guilty hole," exposing "murders, treasons and detested sins" (39–40), making his treacherous cousin Bolingbroke "tremble at his sin" (3.2.48). In this play, the blood of the eventual murder of Richard is clearly associated with the balm or holy oil used in the religious ritual of anointing the monarch at their coronation. To assume kingship, Macbeth has spilt the "sacred" blood of an anointed king and will assume the role of a 'player king' himself when 'invested' at Scone (2.4.38–9). Ironically, however, Richard II's statement about consequences is not entirely proven in that play. Bolingbroke is not "affrighted" by the light of the king or the deed of deposition which follows. Whether balm or blood, the realities appear to depend on political pragmatism rather than on holy protection or the ceremonial trappings in which Richard has so much faith. The guilt-ridden Macbeth, however, is destroyed by political strategy – a union between Scotland and England, with Malcolm resorting to the English for support (4.3.214–17) – although the nature of kingship in this union continues to be articulated in the vocabulary of saintliness. Macduff refers to Malcolm's father as "a most sainted king" and the queen as one who "Died every day she lived" (4.3.123, 125). The king of England, Edward the Confessor, has the power to solicit heaven to cure people of sicknesses, "Hanging a golden stamp about their necks/Put on with holy prayers" (4.3.170–1). This king of England "'tis spoken,/To the succeeding royalty he leaves/The healing benediction. With this strange virtue/He hath a heavenly gift of prophecy,/And sundry blessings hang about his throne/That speak him full of grace" (4.3.171–6). This utilizes the language of the traditional Catholic prayer to the Virgin Mary ("Hail Mary, full of grace, the Lord is with thee"), but is attributed to the king who is watching the play, full of the hypocrisy of his own 'holiness', and, ironically, the man who was responsible for the publication of the 'King James' Bible in 1611. Shakespeare may appear to be flattering King James, but at the same time he may also be teasing out some of the moral issues that inform the play. Much depends on whether we accept an orthodox reading of what the play's surface texture suggests or search underneath that surface to enquire about the foundations of these issues, their structure, and their effects as they emerge in the tragic action.

▶ The playwright's art

Thomas de Quincey's essay 'On the Knocking at the Gate in *Macbeth*'[45] demonstrates Shakespeare's efficacy in manipulating the response of his audience to the forces at work in the play. The knocking at the gate is a sound in the silence following the murder and it is a sign of the beginning of the encroachment of the outside world into the 'hellish' environment of Macbeth's castle. After the Porter's jokes on equivocation, the scene takes on a further dimension. Lennox tells Macbeth of the dreadful weather and strange occurrences of the night, "chimneys ... blown down", "Lamentings heard i'th'air, strange screams of death", "confused events", "the earth/Was feverous and did shake" (2.3.49–55). Macbeth replies simply, "'Twas a rough night" (56). Dramatically, this simplicity is Shakespeare's way of signalling anxiety as the character anticipates Macduff's discovery of the dead King Duncan.

Equivocation appears to be the problem from the very start of the play, when the weird sisters' comment, "Fair is foul, and foul is fair" (1.1.12). It sets the scene and paves the route, along with their further prophecies, for Macbeth's journey and arrival. It leads ultimately to that final recognition of the futility of his actions when he hears of the death of Lady Macbeth:

...Out, out, brief candle.
Life's but a walking shadow, a poor player
That struts and frets his hour upon the stage
And then is heard no more. It is a tale
Told by an idiot, full of sound and fury,
Signifying nothing. (5.5.23–8)

The actor has left the stage, the light of life has gone out like a burnt candle, and all is darkness. Without the natural rhythms of life and the institutions that are designed to support them, royalty is without substance and devoid of meaning. We are as shadows, an image used in *Richard II* (4.1.287) where the king, about to be deposed, also notes "for I must nothing be" (4.1.195). It is akin also to the "We are such stuff/As dreams are made on", a sentiment that Shakespeare places in the mouth of Prospero in *The Tempest* (4.1.169–70). In *Macbeth* we have a poor player, a tale or story written by an idiot, the sound and fury of the tragic actor that culminates in meaninglessness, or does it? Macbeth's "nothing" may reflect the variety of discourses that feed into the play's demonstration of the consequences of equivocation. As Malcolm Evans points out, "The 'nothing' signified is not merely an absence but a delirious plentitude of selves and meanings, always prior to, and in excess of, the self-naturalizing signs and subjects of the discourses it calls perpetually to account"[46]. In that "nothing" is the enigma of a play that at once flatters and questions divine kingship, authority and war, treason, murder and royal succession.

The reverberations of the word 'nothing' extend far beyond the nihilistic confines of *Macbeth*. It surfaces in other Shakespearean contexts, and with modifications in its meanings, but it also points forward to modern minimalist depictions of artistic endeavour. Macbeth does not accept the existential vision of a barren existence emptied of significance as a consequence of human action, but elsewhere in Shakespeare, 'art' is offered as a bulwark against the inevitable ravages of time. In the Sonnets, Shakespeare posits a belief that art itself might outlast the monument of "sluttish time", but in *Macbeth* something else is happening. The character expresses a nihilism that is part of the positivism of the process of the play as it develops. The articulation of the "poor player" on the stage, with his "sound and fury" may signify "nothing" in the sense of having no physical substance, but it points to the existential fact that something can and has indeed come from nothing. It is the reversal of King Lear's "Nothing will come of nothing: speak again". (*King Lear*, 1.1.82) The actors of the play, faced with the nihilistic vision of the protagonist, are constantly encouraged to speak again, making something out of nothing in and through their performances. The 'something' is the play itself expressed, contradictorily, in this great speech that is at one level self-conscious, but whose meanings extend beyond the consciousness of the character, whose perspective is limited by the action in which he is implicated.

However, we cannot say that this is a truth expounded, or an emotion stimulated by the dramatist. The sentiment "full of sound and fury,/Signifying nothing" (5.5.27–8), is talked of by a fictitious character created by a writer telling the tale through the medium of drama. The 'visions' presented are there for entertainment, to stimulate thought and to encourage some understanding of the moral problems that arise in a society caught in the grip of equivocation. In this we have to challenge the kind of criticism that calls for a cathartic effect on the audience's emotions at the end of the play.

During the journey of the play and its manifold complications, Macbeth is shown to hold on to one final 'truth' promised to him. It is an equivocation of the truth of birth itself. He tells Macduff:

I bear a charmèd life, which must not yield
To one of woman born (5.7.49–50)

To which Macduff responds:

Despair thy charm,
And let the angel whom thou still hast served
Tell thee: Macduff was from his mother's womb
Untimely ripped. (5.7.51–4)

Macbeth now designates the weird sisters as:

... juggling fiends no more believed
That palter with us in a double sense,
That keep the word of promise to our ear
And break it to our hope. (5.7.57–60)

He falters once he learns the manner of Macduff's birth, "I'll not fight with thee" (60) but nevertheless he does fight, in order to "try the last" (71) or test the weird sisters' equivocations. In his death Macbeth sinks into that silence, that nothingness, that life emptied of all significance produces. Malcolm wraps the narrative up with probably another historical reference to James I: "thanes and kinsmen,/Henceforth be earls, the first that ever Scotland/In such an honour named" (107–9), and so the play ends by flattering, and why shouldn't it? Plays need to please their audiences. Dramatist and actors need to be paid, not punished.

Equivocation, voyeurism, religious dispute, execution, war, murder, revenge, political expediency, ambition, hypocrisy, promises and selfhood intermingle in this complex play that defies easy definitions. Rather it continues to challenge.

5

Othello (1604)

*Excellent wretch! Perdition
catch my soul,
But I do love thee!
And when I love thee not,
Chaos is come again.*

(3.3.100–2)

Contemporary audiences, actors, directors and critics bring their knowledge and their cultural assumptions and values to the act of interpreting a play's text. This is of particular importance in plays where modern scholars and audiences detect the presence of values that they regard as an anathema, and unacceptable prejudice. The question of anti-Semitism in *The Merchant of Venice* and misogyny in *The Taming of the Shrew* are dealt with in *Shakespeare's Comedies*; here we have to ask, is *Othello* racist?

This chapter will look at the marriage between a blackamoor protagonist, Othello, and a white Venetian, Desdemona, and the role of the 'ensign' or flag-bearer, Iago, within the confines of the Venetian society and its anxieties that comprise the social environment of the play. Shakespeare embeds his characters within a particular society, and invites us not only to look at what this might mean, but also at how the business of producing meanings actually works. If we concentrate on dramatic structure, what emerges is an awareness of a whole series of oppositions developed in the play, and of a process of manipulation into which the audience is drawn by being invited to form judgements that the dramatic characters themselves have prompted. Of course it is the playwright who is manipulating the dramatic characters and audience alike, making available to each different levels of knowledge. This mechanism, which critics have called 'discrepant awareness', is a familiar strategy in the comedies but in the tragedies, and in *Othello* in particular, it is a major source of tragic irony. At the core of the play also is the opposition between 'black' and 'white', and the moral, social and political values that it evokes in a Venice that was, historically, held up to be what we would call a 'multicultural' society. Neil MacGregor has explored the presence of Moors in the London of Shakespeare's time from a historical perspective. He notes the alliance between Elizabeth I and the king of Morocco, both of whom were enemies of Catholic Spain. He records also the reputation the Moroccans had for their wealth in gold[47]. Popular perception of Moors and their political alliances, however, was not always favourable, and as MacGregor shows, there was an antipathy between the two views. Those antagonistic towards Othello "use racial insults against the Moor" but "for all the times he is associated with darkness, Othello is also praised", although, we may note, as a necessary supporter of the Venetian state. MacGregor concludes: "The blacker his antagonists paint him, the more Shakespeare forces his audience to acknowledge Othello's honour and integrity"[48]. While politically Elizabeth I may have favoured the alliance with an enemy of Spain, even if he was a Moor, Julia Briggs provides evidence that the queen was not consistent in her approach[49]. In 1596 she had "ten blackmoors ('of which kind of people there are already here too many')" deported, and also signed an edict to gain the release of 89 prisoners by the exchange of the same number of 'blackamoors'. She urged her subjects to give up Moorish servants in favour of their "own countrymen than ... those kind of people". Briggs observes: "The intolerance of the queen and her officials is even more distressing in view of the fact that most, if not all, of the Africans in England had been brought over by force rather than choice"[50].

Briggs' historical evidence makes it clear that there was racial suspicion and intolerance in Elizabethan and Jacobean society. One of the events celebrating James I's wedding in Oslo (1589) had four black men dancing naked in the snow in front of him and his queen, Anne of Denmark; the men subsequently died of the cold. Black people were servants, entertainers, prostitutes. Briggs observes that this was the beginning of the prejudice associating beauty with pale skin: black skin was the result of exposure to the sun, and hence, in an agricultural economy, an indication of low social status and an animalistic sexual energy.

▶ Racism

'Black' and 'white' are adjectives we now try to avoid using to describe human physical characteristics because they carry with them negative racist overtones. As we saw in Chapter 4, the darkness of the night is a setting for evil deeds. Lady Macbeth makes this point in her invocation "Come, thick night,/And pall thee in the dunnest smoke of hell, ... /Nor heaven peep through the blanket of the dark" (1.5.48–51). The vocabulary she uses infuses her thoughts with a powerful moral charge that reinforces the criminal nature of what is about to happen. Macbeth's first words echo those of the weird sisters, "So foul and fair a day I have not seen" (1.3.39). The play exposes the equivocation in which foul is made to look fair, but there is a wider context for it. Shakespeare's Sonnet 147 concludes by drawing a relationship between darkness, evil, the night and hell:

For I have sworn thee fair and thought thee bright,
Who art as black as hell, as dark as night.

Certainly in Shakespeare's play, the colour of Othello's skin is deployed, particularly in the opening scenes, by the flag-bearer Iago to promote a prejudiced opinion of the military leader. Shakespeare provides Iago with coarse, descriptive language, including in the description of Othello's recent marriage to Desdemona: "Even now, now, very now, an old black ram/Is tupping your white ewe" (1.1.92–3). Iago's intent here is to prey upon a Venetian anxiety that, for an early Jacobean audience, might have existed under the surface of the apparent order and freedom of the 'ideal' republic:

... Arise, arise!
Awake the snorting citizens with the bell,
Or else the devil will make a grandsire of you.
Arise, I say! (1.1.93–6)

Desdemona's father, Brabantio, reacts against the union of the two lovers, accusing Othello of using magic to entrap his daughter. But note also in the passage above Iago's language of contempt – "snorting citizens", "the devil" – and the fact that the word "arise" is endowed with a sexual force. Shakespeare creates in Iago a figure who uses obscenity as a means of expression and who reduces his adversaries to the level of animals. The reason for his success for most of the play is that he preys upon fears and anxieties with which his victims identify: Brabantio is anxious about his daughter, as any patriarch would be, and that anxiety spreads to fears of miscegenation, a prejudice that lurks underneath the surface of Venice and that Iago mobilizes as he pursues his evil scheme.

The play expresses clear racial attitudes, but that does not necessarily make it a racist play, or one that promotes racism. Talking of the violence in his plays, the dramatist Edward Bond writes about portraying it naturally because "People who do not want writers to write about violence want to stop them writing about us and our time. It would be immoral not to write about violence"[51]. For Bond, violence must be confronted, must be treated critically, socially and ethically if society is to be improved. Modern theatre similarly needs more performances that deal with racism. That may be a legitimate way for the 21st century to mobilize an early 17th-century text, and in his rewriting of Shakespeare's *King Lear* Bond has accomplished that.

▶ The outsider

Shakespeare isn't necessarily political in the sense that he sought to propound a particular thesis. His dramatic purpose was, as Bond also tells us, to ask questions, and in *Othello* he does exactly that. Factually he would, probably, have known that the Venetian republic depended for its defence on mercenary soldiers. Outsiders were appointed because Venice was a trading republic and not a military state. For Shakespeare, one of the play's literary sources, a novella first published in 1565, stimulated an imaginative prospect: what if this prominent outsider fell in love with a daughter of a member of the Venetian ruling class and married her? If at the same time Venice were to be in danger, how would the politicians react? Would they support the father of the woman or would they try to appease him? The hypocrisy of government was as much a subject for theatrical exploitation in Shakespeare's day as it is now. While necessary, the outsider would be tolerated whatever he had done – and in this play we are never quite sure what he has done since the dramatist implies that the father at first encouraged the relationship with his daughter (1.3.142f.). Make the outsider black but with a 'white' heart and the dramatic potential is even greater. We might now consider there to be a clear issue of racism here, but for this practitioner of the theatre 400 years ago the matter raised different but equally serious concerns. *Othello* intensifies a theme Shakespeare had developed before in other contexts; the resonances of skin colour go back to the much earlier *Titus Andronicus* (1591–4), which even today continues to prove controversial.

In *The Merchant of Venice* and in *The Taming of the Shrew*, the outsider, discrimination and conflict are seen as ingredients for drama. So too with *Othello*, a play that confirms the underlying structure of problems, journeys, arrivals, complications and silence noted elsewhere. The problem is threefold. First, Othello, the outsider, has secretly married Brabantio's daughter, Desdemona. Secondly, the Turks are attacking the Venetian island of Cyprus. Thirdly, there is the malevolence of Iago towards the general, allegedly as a result of being passed over for promotion. The journey takes the protagonist to Cyprus, and to the frontier where the Turkish fleet is destroyed. One problem has been solved but others remain. It is on this frontier that Iago weaves his plot to destroy Othello with jealousy, and he succeeds to the point where Desdemona is publicly abused and finally murdered. The scene of her death begins with an erroneous self-justification that involves an appeal for justice in a nameless cause. But herein lies the complication. The actual self-knowledge or *anagnorisis* occurs only after Desemona has been killed, and it is followed by the protagonist's own characterization of the problem in terms of a confrontation between a "Venetian" and a "turbaned Turk" that results in his own death by suicide. The "hellish" agent of the destruction, meanwhile, remains steadfastly silent but it is expected that torture will loosen his tongue, "The time, the place, the torture: O, enforce it!" (5.2.414). Of course, when Iago next speaks, the play will begin again, rather like the tale that Horatio is entrusted with at the end of *Hamlet*. The play advertises its future performances.

▶ Two significant statements

Iago: *I am not what I am* (1.1.67)
Desdemona: *I saw Othello's visage in his mind* (1.3.267)

The portrayal of Iago's evil is a narrative element operating throughout the play whether the setting is Venice or

Cyprus. There has been much debate, particularly since the early 19th century, about Iago's motive for what he does. Coleridge coined the term 'motiveless malignity' to explain his behaviour. But that debate leads us into the Bradlean fallacy which endows a fictional character with a human reality. Of course in rehearsal, actors like to find a persona. E. A. J. Honigmann may be useful to actors here in his distinction between the motiveless malignity and the character's 'contemptuousness'. He refers to the passage at 1.3.375ff:

> ... I hate the Moor:
> And it is thought abroad that 'twixt my sheets
> He has done my office: I know not if't be true,
> But I, for mere suspicion in that kind,
> Will do as if for surety.

The speech concludes:

> The Moor is of a free and open nature,
> That thinks men honest that but seem to be so,
> And will as tenderly be led by th'nose
> As asses are.
> I have't: it is engend'red: hell and night
> Must bring this monstrous birth to the world's light.

What may interest us further is that it is the white man, Iago, who is summoning hell and night. The conflict between fair and foul is not initially, or indeed ultimately, between Othello and Desdemona, but between Othello and Iago. It might have been expected in the 17th century that the black man would be the evil one, as with Aaron the Moor in *Titus Andronicus*, but Shakespeare has manipulated our expectations by reversing them, while at the same time mobilizing what in Jacobean England were popular prejudices.

The matter is further complicated since it is the 'white' Iago, and not the 'black' Othello who initially harbours sexual fantasies; in Iago's case the possibility of adultery between his wife, Emilia, and Othello (2.1.279–83). Shakespeare provides a variety of totally unproven but plausible 'facts' by which Iago justifies his destruction of the general. In the opening scene Iago's evil is laid bare with a statement that exposes the perverse nature of evil as the antithesis of God; in the Old Testament of the Bible, the name of God is not to be uttered, but when he speaks he says "I am, what I am". In Iago's revelation to Rodorigo[52] of his enmity towards Othello, he says that he is not transparent because transparency would involve wearing his heart upon his sleeve "For daws to peck at: I am not what I am" (1.1.66–7); in other words, I have the capacity to deceive in that I invert my appearance and what it signifies; I am an 'ensign' who can "show out a flag and sign of love,/Which is indeed but sign" (1.1.165–6). In this scene Iago is being 'honest' with both his onstage audience and the theatre audience in describing what will be a hidden dishonesty in the narrative. His statement, in being the denial of God's name, links his presence with the devil, even though, as emphasized earlier, Iago is white and Othello is black.

Bernard Spivack explored the origins of the dramatic characterization of the 'devil' Iago in the tradition of the medieval figure of Vice[53]. 'Vice' is a devil figure who appears in such medieval plays as *Mankind* or *Mundus et Infans*, to tempt Mankind into sin and towards hell.

As a generalized allegorical figure of all humanity, Mankind in these plays is always saved at the end of the drama. By the late 16th century such stereotypes had become to some extent secularized and individualized, as in Marlowe's *Dr Faustus* (1592?), where Faustus is characterized as an individual who has sold his soul to the devil, and in the end he isn't saved like Mankind but taken to hell. The devil figure of temptation, Mephistopheles, who is also given a modicum of individuality, triumphs.

▲ Willard White (Othello) and Ian McKellen (Iago) in a 1989 RSC production.

Venice was known as the city of trade, Moors for their wealth in gold. In *The Merchant of Venice*, one of Portia's wooers is a Moor who in the casket scene chooses gold but by doing so loses the woman he wishes to marry. In *Othello*, the Moor is shown to have won the woman not through competition or wealth but through the eloquence of his strange, enchanting tales:

Of moving accidents by flood and field,
Of hair-breadth scapes i'th'imminent deadly breach,
Of being taken by the insolent foe
And sold to slavery, ...
And of the cannibals that each other eat,
The Anthropophagi and men whose heads
Grew beneath their shoulders. (1.3.149–52, 157–9)

It was these images, histories, which had attracted Desdemona and the speech as a whole may well have encouraged Shakespeare's audience to look past Othello's physical appearance. Martin Wine comments, "The speech reflects a harmony between language and psyche that moves – or should move – Othello's listeners to look, indeed, beyond the *signs* of discourse and of skin colour to see the 'visage in his mind' that Desdemona saw."[54] Stephen Greenblatt observes that it is Iago who is "the improviser, the manipulator of signs that bear no resemblance to what they profess to signify – but it is Othello himself who is ... (the) one (that) can win pity for oneself only by becoming a tale of oneself, and hence by ceasing to be oneself"[55]; while Wine holds that, "Iago as playwright uses language to imprison characters: Shakespeare, however, uses it to set them free in all their mysterious individuality and thereby strengthens our sense of reality"[56]. Iago is one of those Shakespearean individuals whom we see fashioning himself, albeit in a particularly malicious manner. Desdemona, on the other hand, is explicit in describing the nature of her love for Othello; her statement that "I saw Othello's visage in his mind" (1.3.267) prompts us to bring all these points together since it contextually implies that, first, this is a meeting of two minds, in contradiction to the popular claim that the Moor and the woman are stereotypically associated primarily with sexual lust. Secondly, the difference of visage between them has the potential for tragedy because it is these stereotypes that will be developed through Iago's plotting. Thirdly, Desdemona's elopement signals a wilfulness, if not an individuality, that Iago proceeds to exploit to destroy her and Othello. So while Iago may have antecedents in the Vice figure of medieval drama, this is very much a Renaissance play in which the notion of individual choice is portrayed as having evolved from within a particular society. Iago is a secularized construct portrayed as baiting Othello, and combining both stereotype and individual. The emphasis on stereotype is, nonetheless, just sufficient to make Desdemona's claimed infidelity plausible, exposing the ease with which people can be deceived as well as revealing the tragic consequences of that deception.

▶ Being drawn into the play

The fact that Iago is given these two personae to weave his manipulative web is the means by which Shakespeare makes him more credible. He draws us further into the story with the exchange with Rodorigo, who helps Iago to fabricate a case against Desdemona which we know to be untrue but also plausible. Iago first plants with Rodorigo the idea of Desdemona's alleged adultery with Cassio; Rodorigo is initially incredulous:

Rodorigo: *I cannot believe that in her: she's full of the most blessed condition.*

Iago: *Blessed fig's-end! The wine she drinks is made of grapes. If she had been blessed, she would never have loved the Moor. Blessed pudding! Didst thou not see her paddle with the palm of his hand? Didst not mark that?*

Rodorigo: *Yes, that I did, but that was but courtesy.*

Iago: *Lechery, by this hand: an index and obscure prologue to the history of lust and foul thoughts.* (2.1.245–51)

We may know that what Iago is saying is false, and we are not being duped like the fictional Rodorigo, but we are being drawn into the fiction by being asked to make the kinds of judgements we see the characters making, albeit from a more knowledgeable position. The danger we face is that we may be persuaded to accept some of the judgements influenced by racism and misogyny that we see the characters making. Moreover, we should not confuse what the dramatic characters say with what the play says. For example, Catherine Belsey warns:

> *In written works it matters who addresses whom, in what situation and with what authority. When the works in question are fictional, it matters that we differentiate between the fictional speaker and the text. The views of the villain are probably contrary to what the audience is invited to believe: Iago's racism and misogyny … should not necessarily be taken for the play's.*[57]

This is true, but periodically throughout the play Iago seeks to attract the audience to his perspective by taking it into his confidence. Shortly after the exchange with

Rodorigo, for example, Iago addresses the audience directly, enticing them momentarily into his machinations:

> *That Cassio loves her, I do well believe 't:*
> *That she loves him, 'tis apt and of great credit.*
> *The Moor – howbeit that I endure him not –*
> *Is of a constant, loving, noble nature* (2.1.270ff.)

This individualized secular figure invites the spectators on the stage and in the theatre into his confidence, thus setting up a bridge between the fictional world that the play creates and the extra-theatrical reality of the audience. In this he certainly resembles the medieval figure of Vice, attracting and amusing spectators, inviting their complicity and diverting them with comedy. Shakespeare has created a confidence trickster that the audience may well find attractive. He doesn't have a clear motive, but those he does reveal are always plausible. His appeals to the audience are, however, part of the complex web of suggestion and persuasion that involves questions of proof and the manipulation of evidence; indeed, it is no accident that there are issues of 'truth' and 'falsehood' that even the audience fails to resolve. For example, what has led up to Desdemona's elopement? What has her father done to encourage the relationship between her and Othello? Who is Bianca? What is her relationship with Cassio? In short, we are asked to go through the same process of evaluating evidence as Rodorigo, Brabantio, Cassio and finally Othello. In fact, only the Duke of Venice behaves correctly, withholding judgement about the destination of the Turkish fleet until he has received all of the evidence about its strategic movements.

Even when audiences reflect on Othello's tragic error in accepting Iago's story about the whereabouts and destiny of Desdemona's handkerchief as proof of her infidelity, they remain within the frame of the illusory world Shakespeare has created. William Empson in his essay 'Honest in Othello'[58] has noted over 50 uses of the word 'honesty' or 'honest' in the play. They all help to draw us into engagement with the rhetorical process of constructing and suggesting meanings, in a similar way to Mark Antony's subtle manipulation of his onstage audience in *Julius Caesar* (1599). By a series of repetitions and inferences the treachery of Brutus is insinuated, so that the description of the conspirators as "honourable men" (*Julius Caesar*, 3.2.70f.) becomes increasingly hollow. *Othello* adds a further twist to this subtlety since the audience, unlike the characters, knows how hollow the epithet 'honest' is when applied to Iago.

Shakespeare gives a degree of humanity both to Iago, and to Othello. Othello is given a dignity and authority in that the language he uses is in marked contrast to the sneering calumnious language of Iago. The linguistic difference is evident in Act 1 Scene 2 when Brabantio, Rodorigo and others come armed to take Othello to the duke. He politely asserts control:

> *Keep up your bright swords, for the dew will rust them.*
> *Good signior, you shall more command with years*
> *Than with your weapons* (1.2.71–3)

In the Venetian court, Othello uses an elevated but studied rhetorical language; notice, for example, that his explanation of the situation is in a language which is carefully measured:

> *Most potent, grave and reverend signiors,*
> *My very noble and approved good masters:*
> *That I have ta'en away this old man's daughter,*
> *It is most true: true I have married her;*
> *The very head and front of my offending*
> *Hath this extent, no more* (1.3.86–91)

By Act 4 Scene 1, however, Iago has destroyed Othello's dignity, his control, his calm authority, as he had done earlier with Brabantio:

> *Lie with her? Lie on her? We say 'Lie on her' when they belie her ... It is not words that shake me thus. Pish! Noses, ears and lips. Is't possible? Confess? Handkerchief? O devil!* [*Falls in a trance.*] (4.1.42, 46–7)

Othello now speaks in a disfunctional prose before collapsing in the tortured silence of a trance. Iago, however, continues to confide in the audience: "My medicine works! Thus credulous fools are caught" (4.1.49), inviting us to share his outlook. Othello's dilemma becomes ours as we are forced to divide our attention between the diabolically successful Iago and the 'noble Moor', who has now been reduced to the status of a victim. The audience's reaction at this point is often mixed; some react with laughter and embarrassment at the melodrama, others with 'pity' for the victim. The action is so subtly developed that this scene causes actors serious difficulty in trying to locate the right tone for the performance. The actor portraying Othello here has to strike a fine balance. Similarly the audience is required to experience vicariously what is being communicated to them indirectly via the characters. A number of what we might call 'conversations' are going on simultaneously in this, one of the most complex and conversational of all Shakespeare's plays.

One issue which has interested critics, commentators and theatre practitioners alike is the question of who the protagonist is in *Othello*. Is it Iago, or Othello, or both? Martin Wine discusses the relationship in 20th-century productions between the two characters, noting, however, that:

> *We cannot be sure how Iago was played in Shakespeare's day. Possibly he ... was hissed and booed as a Machiavellian villain. But there seems no doubt that Richard Burbage's Othello, remembered and praised long after his death, was not too small for the Globe stage. We do not know who his Iago was.*[59]

Wine notes two contrasting 20th-century interpretations. The National Theatre production in 1960 deliberately subordinated Frank Finlay's bluff Iago to Laurence Olivier's powerful but heavy racialized Othello, an interpretation based on F. R. Leavis's view that the protagonist is the real agent of his downfall. By contrast, the RSC's 1971 production with Emrys James as Iago and Brewster Mason as Othello allowed the villainous manipulator of the play to subordinate the play's tragedy to comedy, becoming, as Frank Marcus noted in his review, "the tragic-comedy of Iago"[60].

Both Olivier's and Mason's performances were in the old tradition, with white actors blacking up to play the role. But the play seems to exude an even greater power when black actors assume the role; notable past performances include Paul Robeson and James Earl Jones in the USA and more recently the opera singer Willard White (RSC, 1989) and Adrian Lester (National Theatre, 2013). The answer to the question is that a balance has to be found as one actor plays off the other in the context of the directorial choices that have been made. What is important is that the one does not undermine the significance of the other, and that the interpretation of the whole is a coherent one.

Shakespeare creates in *Othello* a play of fall, of victimization and of manipulation. He exposes what we may now call a racist, and depicts the domesticity of a love being led to destruction, with the protagonist-turned-murderer asking pitifully, "Where should Othello go?" (5.2.308) There is nowhere for him to go. It is Iago, ironically, who takes a vow of silence: "From this time forth I never will speak word" (5.2.342). He is, as Greenblatt says, "cut off from original motive and final disclosure. The only termination possible in his case is not revelation but silence"[61]. Silence is silence but the causes of silence vary. As Wine succinctly expresses it, Iago's retreat into silence places him: "once and for all outside the pale of humanity"[62].

In contrast, Shakespeare almost parodies his sad creation of the Moor, who calls for quiet before embarking on a rhetorical tour de force: "Soft you; a word or two before you go" (5.2.381). The "soft you" calls for the audience's attention as much as it does for that of the characters on stage:

Speak of me as I am: nothing extenuate,
Nor set down aught in malice. Then must you speak
Of one that loved not wisely but too well:
Of one not easily jealous, but being wrought,
Perplexed in the extreme; of one whose hand,
... threw a pearl away
Richer than all his tribe (5.2.385–91)

The protagonist here is giving an epilogue before killing himself. Shakespeare is still tempting us to question, to judge. Do we agree or disagree? Is this what we have witnessed? Is this a perverse judgement that Othello is now seeking to make right? Of course, in dramatic terms the active protagonist cannot be allowed to sink into inactivity. Othello's ending is a dramatization of the main conflict in the play, and it is one that is geographically located on a frontier between the ideal republic (Venice) and her hostile adversary (the Turks):

And say besides, that in Aleppo once,
Where a malignant and a turbaned Turk
Beat a Venetian and traduced the state,
I took by th'throat the circumcisèd dog
And smote him, thus. (5.2.395–9)

Shakespeare portrays Othello the outsider as acting for Venice to the last, executing himself as he had done her traditional 'malignant' enemy. We may wonder if, through the machinations of the Iago character, Shakespeare may have been prompting us to consider still whether this fictional black man was himself a victim of the Venetian state or whether, as he says, a figure who "loved not wisely but too well". In a world still riven by racial and religious conflict, it is for us to decide, for us to reconsider, as it will be for the generations that follow.

6

Conclusion: Language and soliloquy

It is the cause, it is the cause, my soul:
Let me not name it to you, you chaste stars:
It is the cause.

Othello (5.2.1-3)

Poetry is an essential element of Shakespeare's craftsmanship. Some literary criticism influenced by Romanticism has tended to regard it as though it were like the bark on a tree. Touch the poetry and you find the play. It is, of course, fundamental and, along with structure, plot, character and theme, forms the shape of a Shakespearean play. The text is a dramatic score, and poetry helps to make the play work. This chapter will consider how it does so, in particular through an examination of the use of the soliloquies in the four great tragedies. But poetry is not the only form of language used in the plays; prose similarly contributes to the structuring of the plays, and provides necessary contrasts while also giving insights into dramatic purpose and artistic design.

The usual poetic metre, the ten-beat line (iambic pentameter), is frequently varied by the dramatist for particular purposes, while the poetic medium generally is used to create environment and ambience, playing on the audience's imagination. Poetry contrasts with prose for particular circumstances, sometimes in relation to the social station of the characters. We have already examined the way this works in the case of Iago, who can reduce the otherwise eloquent Othello to prose gibbering. The Gravedigger in Act 5 Scene 1 of *Hamlet* speaks in prose but so does Hamlet, even at times when he is reflecting on the issues of life's transcience, death and states of feeling. In the gravedigging scene, Hamlet's famous reflection on the state of the dead court jester – "Alas, poor Yorick! I knew him, Horatio: a fellow of infinite jest, of most excellent fancy" (5.1.141ff.) – is spoken in prose. Similarly, prose is used in the earlier discussion with Rosencrantz and Guildenstern, often regarded as a key moment in the play, when they are trying to find out the reason for Hamlet's melancholy but are refusing to say why they have come to court:

I will tell you why; so shall my anticipation prevent your discovery, and your secrecy to the king and queen moult no feather. I have of late – but wherefore I know not – lost all my mirth, forgone all custom of exercise; and indeed it goes so heavily with my disposition that this goodly frame, the earth, seems to me a sterile promontory, this most excellent canopy, the air, look you, this brave o'erhanging firmament, this majestical roof fretted with golden fire, why, it appears no other thing to me than a foul and pestilent congregation of vapours. What a piece of work is a man! How noble in reason, how infinite in faculty, in form and moving how express and admirable, in action how like an angel, in apprehension how like a god! The beauty of the world, the paragon of animals – and yet, to me, what is this quintessence of dust? Man delights not me – no, nor woman neither, though by your smiling you seem to say so.
(2.2.277–88)

This is a very sinuous prose that verges on poetry. Some regard its use here as offering an insight into or an expression of Hamlet's character, but we may notice that he is talking with two characters who are not to be trusted. It certainly complements the soliloquies in the play, which are revelatory of character and of theme. It is fruitless to speculate about why Shakespeare uses prose on these occasions, except perhaps that by doing so the effect is to reduce the status of Rosencrantz and

Guildenstern, and expose their unsuccessful attempts to find out what Hamlet calls, in a later prose passage, "the heart of my mystery", (3.2.313–4). These characters, symptoms of a disordered state, are unworthy of poetry, just as in much of his 'madness' or weariness Hamlet's own disordered mental state is also communicated in prose.

Yet there is another aspect to this "I will tell you why" passage. At Act 2 Scene 2 lines 277–88 Hamlet is also interacting with his audience: the "sterile promontory" is the Elizabethan thrust stage on which the actor is walking, and its canopy of sun and signs of the zodiac the "majestical roof fretted with golden fire". This takes the character out into the audience itself, so he is surrounded by spectators standing around the stage, perhaps even calling out to the player as he insults them as "a foul and pestilent congregation of vapours". This 'reality' replete with its range of social types is in stark contrast to the 'man' who is "noble in reason", "infinite in faculty" and whom Hamlet impersonates as the true Renaissance prince. But irrespective of their identities, whether popular auditor or Renaissance prince, they are all destined to become a "quintessence of dust" (2.2.287). The choice of the word "quintessence", referring to perfection of form but now associated with 'dust', is exquisitely nihilistic. In this instance, prose can be used to deflate but in doing so it can also be used to inflate the significance of a particular line.

Words are carefully chosen by the dramatist to open his plays, setting tone or atmosphere as in the following openings:

Macbeth
First Witch: *When shall we three meet again?*
  In thunder, lightning, or in rain?
Second Witch: *When the hurly-burly's done,*
  When the battle's lost and won.

King Lear
Kent: *I thought the king had more affected the Duke of Albany than Cornwall.*

Othello
Rodorigo: *Never tell me! I take it much unkindly*
  That thou, Iago, who hast had my purse
  As if the strings were thine, shouldst know of this.

Hamlet
Barnardo: *Who's there?*

Each of these openings grabs our attention with a statement that to some extent expresses much of the play itself. The conundrums of the weird sisters pervade *Macbeth*, leading him to test their last equivocal prophecy before his death. The puzzlement at the king's actions in *King Lear* demonstrates a changeable, confused mind that will descend into madness and destruction. So much is to be taken "unkindly" in *Othello*, a play in which no-one triumphs. "Who's there?" is a fundamental question reiterated throughout *Hamlet*. Most of these openings are *in medias res* (into the middle of a narrative), giving the impression of joining something that is already in progress. They also create atmosphere, as in *Richard III*, one of the most well-known openings of all:

Richard: *Now is the winter of our discontent*
Made glorious summer by this son of York:

The emphasis on the present, "Now", still looks back historically and yet also looks forward to the mischief to come. Laurence Olivier's relishing of the word "Now" in the film version of the play has made it one of the most quoted lines of Shakespeare. In the 1992 RSC production, Simon Russell Beale entered the stage in darkness, with a persistent tap, tap, tap until on the word "Now" he turned on a light and we saw him standing alone with his walking stick. By the use of these devices, the audience are caught by the opening and taken into the play from the start.

The language of the play serves a dramatic function. The poetry that dominates not only reflects philosophical ideas and themes, but deliberately communicates a variety of emotions. E. A. J. Honigmann demonstrates, for example, how in *Hamlet* the dramatist uses a technique whereby one judgement supersedes another to produce a layered effect. He writes: "the audience's judgement of Hamlet's judgement, ... I take to be *the* response-problem of the play. Hamlet assesses or judges the Ghost, Claudius, Gertrude and society at large; the audience judges Hamlet judging the Ghost etc., and in doing so has in effect the same task as Hamlet, at one remove.[63]

This is the peculiar effect produced particularly by the soliloquies, most of which are attributed to Hamlet, although three significant soliloquies, two short and one long, are given to Claudius. Claudius' long soliloquy,

▲ Rory Kinnear as Hamlet in a 2010 National Theatre production.

"O, my offence is rank, it smells to heaven" (3.3.39f.) is a confession of guilt which only the theatre audience hears. It confirms the audience's belief that what the Ghost has said is true and thereby allows the audience to sympathise with Hamlet's intention to kill Claudius, although the fact that he appears to be at prayer raises an interesting moral question. Claudius despairs because he cannot repent, with the result that despite his request for angels to "help" him, he remains in a state as "black as death". Hamlet arrives on the scene to find an opportunity to kill the king but does not do so because he might send Claudius' soul to "heaven". He exits the stage while the king confirms to the audience that his sin is such that he would not receive forgiveness. The audience's response is to be caught between two extremes, a position that momentarily places them in an even more complicated position than the prevaricating Hamlet. These two soliloquies, that of the king and Hamlet's "Now might I do it pat, now he is praying" (76f.), offer the audience two perspectives. They then augment these with a third, since it is with the audience that the proscription on 'revenge' lies. Claudius deserves to die, but Hamlet is in danger of sweeping away the moral prohibition that usually accompanies revenge and that Laertes will disregard when he returns to confront Claudius in Act 4 Scene 4.

Another example of a soliloquy demanding audience speculation and reflection, comes with Othello's great speech, "It is the cause, it is the cause, my soul" (5.2.1–22). The opening lines are a puzzle and they grab our attention. "It is" should be a definitive statement. The word 'it' usually refers to facts: "It is raining", "It is the tragedy called *Othello*." But "It is the cause" makes us ask 'What is the cause?' Is the cause Othello's justification of what he is about to do, and if so, what is that justification? The soliloquy continues by denying that he will "shed her blood". So this is not revenge in the context of 'shedding of blood' nor, we are told, will he "scar" her skin, white and "smooth as monumental alabaster". Is Othello attempting to transform a living being into a statue? Othello looks to a candle which he is to extinguish and compares that act with putting out the light of life. He talks of Prometheus, who in Greek mythology is responsible for mankind's creation but also for stealing for humans the fire of heaven. A restorative fire is denied in Othello's case as a means of bringing back to life the wife he is about to kill. He confirms himself as an agent of "Justice", wishing both to kill Desdemona and to be able still to love her after her death, but he refuses to "name" the cause: "Let me not name it to you, you chaste stars". The soliloquy toys with Othello's fictitious rationale but also elicits a response from the audience, which knows of Desdemona's innocence and understands why Othello's cause must remain nameless. During the process, Desdemona wakes but only to die, while the audience is all the while caught between the intensity of the protagonist's feeling and the injustice of his action. In this way the fictional Othello can persuade us to forget for the moment that we are watching a play, but although the action is not 'real', we are also persuaded, for the moment, to believe in the irreversibility of the protagonist's action.

In the first act of *Macbeth*, the protagonist has an 'aside' which functions like a soliloquy. Shakespeare has his character reflect on the temptation to murder. It shows an anxiety of conscience but also that evil decisions can be justified by reflection upon the deeds themselves. The last few lines are enigmatic:

> *My thought, whose murder yet is but fantastical,*
> *Shakes so my single state of man*
> *That function is smothered in surmise,*
> *And nothing is, but what is not.* (1.3.149–52)

Here, Shakespeare is teasing his audience into an understanding of what is happening. The use of the word "murder" is presented in a challenging context. Is it his thought of "murder" which is "fantastical" or is it his "thought", his conscience and fears that are to be 'murdered'? The language of this speech is in danger of negating itself, as in the final line "and nothing is, but what is not", where the inefficacy of language is communicated through language. This is another version of the "Fair is foul, and foul is fair" motif that runs throughout the play.

Contrast this with Lady Macbeth's great soliloquy, the second half of which begins, "The raven himself is hoarse" (1.5.36–52). There is no enigmatic toing and froing either in language or in her determination:

... Come, thick night,
And pall thee in the dunnest smoke of hell,
That my keen knife see not the wound it makes,
Nor heaven peep through the blanket of the dark.
To cry 'Hold, hold!' (1.5.48–52)

The negative image of night is nicely balanced by the image of the blanket that offers warmth and protection from the cold. In this speech, Lady Macbeth is shown to be of the night. The first invocation of her soliloquy starts with the word "Come", an invitation to be possessed by "spirits" that act as attendants on "mortal thoughts". In darkness ill deeds are done. But there is another aspect to the soliloquy: its full flow is interrupted by a messenger (1.5.25). In the first half of the soliloquy she has reflected on the weakness of Macbeth, the "milk of human kindness" that makes him resist self-advancement through evil. There is harking back perhaps to the Adam and Eve myth, of Satan tempting man through the agency of the female temptress, except that here Lady Macbeth is fully empowered in the service of evil. In the second half, although she calls for herself to be unsexed, the images and their intensity in performance can be highly sexually charged, as they were in Judi Dench's famous portrayal, opposite to Ian McKellen, in 1976. Words such as "blood", "access", "passage", "compunctious visitings", build up to the denial of femininity but in a sexually violent, even sado-masochistic, way: "Come to my woman's breasts/And take my milk for gall, you murd'ring ministers" (1.5.45–6).

There is a reversal of the truth of the body itself, as the sustaining milk of life becomes the life-destroying bitter gall. In this statement of evil, the actress may find elements in the darkness of the human psyche that might augment and sustain her interpretation. Harriet Walter playing opposite Anthony Sher's Macbeth in 2000–1, delivered the speech in a much colder, more calculating way than Judi Dench. Both variations were equally horrifying, and equally challenging.

Shakespeare's art is to allow actors to deploy their own imaginative resources to make the characters live. But through the language he teases the audience. As Act 1 Scene 5 comes to a close, the word "Tomorrow" features:

Lady Macbeth: *And when goes* [Duncan] *hence?*
Macbeth: *Tomorrow, as he purposes.*
Lady Macbeth: *O, never*
    Shall sun that morrow see! (1.5.59-62)

This is one of the triumphs of poetry; it permits the planting in our minds of images that are repeated as the play progresses towards "Tomorrow, and tomorrow, and tomorrow,/Creeps in this petty pace from day to day" (5.5.19–20). The word 'tomorrow' gathers new meaning with repetition, first pointing to an actual 'tomorrow', but then to another less specific, more terrifyingly vague notion of a future with no meaning that will end by "signifying nothing".

Macbeth's great soliloquy: "If it were done when 'tis done, then 'twere well/It were done quickly" (1.7.1–28) presses forward for six and a half lines before it comes to a full rest. Then it continues with a conjunction, "But in these cases". The first lines are almost a tongue-twister ending in a desire for things to happen "quickly". The form of the speech works both with and against the substance of the speech. The character speaks quickly but cannot get to the end of the thought process. So the rhythm of the language expresses that very process. The substance of the speech bears out Lady Macbeth's reservations earlier. Here we are shown that Macbeth is someone who has a conscience, someone who balances virtue against anarchic desire. But Shakespeare is relentless in keeping before us the image of a baby. Pity is like "a naked new-born babe" (1.7.21) which earlier Lady Macbeth would have fed with "gall", not "milk" (1.5.46). The image of the innocent babe goes right through the play, as do the images of night and of sleep: Macbeth says he thought he'd heard a voice crying "Macbeth does murder sleep" (2.2.43), and Lady Macbeth is given no rest in the 'sleep walking' scene (5.1).

In *Macbeth* we see the mind playing tricks on itself, the dagger appearing in front of the would-be murderer

(2.1.40f.) and later Banquo's ghost appearing at the feast (3.4), examples of the way in which both the anticipation and the memory of horror are communicated in the play. This is part of what we might now call the gothic horror element of *Macbeth*, produced by all kinds of visual effects in today's technologically sophisticated theatre, but produced originally by Shakespeare through language. His characters, their actions, their environment, their debates are created through an ordering of words, creating images and impressions uttered by and embodied in actors. His was mainly an aural medium, although there were stage props, costumes and thunder sheets etc. But in Shakespearean drama it is mostly the words that create the experience and carry the emotion of the drama.

Creating Christian art in a Christian context has a linguistic significance in itself: "In the beginning was the Word, and the Word was with God, and the Word was God" is the opening verse of St John's Gospel in the Bible. In Christianity, the "Word" is the start of "being" itself. The metaphysical question of being or not being is the subject of probably the most famous soliloquy of all, "To be, or not to be, that is the question" (*Hamlet*, 3.1.62f.), a question with which we have some empathy. We understand the dilemma facing the prince, perhaps because it is a question that remains current. The difference between life and death is of interest to all of us, in all historical epochs, so even though we know that behind the dramatic character is an actor, we suspend our disbelief because what the character says strikes a chord with us individually as human beings and collectively as a theatre audience. The soliloquy goes on to ask whether there is a life after death or not, whether there is a reason for us being here, whether there is a point to being alive. As such, the soliloquy takes the form of a Socratic debate, posing questions that the play goes on to explore.

There are five great soliloquies in the Folio edition of *Hamlet*, with a sixth included in Q2. One means of discussing the play is to take each and see how they accelerate us through the narrative. The opening words of each are worth paying attention to:

O, that this too too solid flesh would melt, (1.2.129)
... Now I am alone.
O, what a rogue and peasant slave am I! (2.2.480)
To be, or not to be, that is the question: (3.1.62)
'Tis now the very witching time of night, (3.2.331)
Now might I do it pat, now he is praying: (3.3.76)

and from the Second Quarto:

How all occasions do inform against me, (following 4.3.9, line 105f., p. 2002)

Two of the openings are not even words but a single letter, "O", a vocative expressing an emotion from within. "'Tis" is the affirmative "It is". "Now" is also affirmative. "How" usually asks a question but here is rhetorical and therefore affirmative, and "To" introduces the metaphysical question "To be, or not to be". Each opening word puts us into the character's dilemma, action, fictional existence, his personal questioning or affirmation of a moment, but also a growing affirmation of control over the play, pushing the action forward through the character's fictional meditation and reflections. These soliloquies act as a spine for the main character's performance. Ben Kingsley, talking privately about playing the role in 1975, said he structured his entire demeanour in the role around that spine, giving an indication of how a great actor approaches the evolving task of playing Hamlet.

Shakespeare's plays don't matter in the way that air or water matter. They are not essential for life itself, although for many they do matter in the experience of life because they create a process of debate which continues after the play is over. This despite Shakespeare's constant warnings that the play is but a play, an imitation of things of life. I drew *Shakespeare's Comedies* to a close with a particular line which I will repeat here as it is applicable to discussion of the tragedies: "If this were played upon a stage now, I could condemn it as an improbable fiction" (*Twelfth Night*, 3.4.97–8). But we do not. Instead we reflect on these constructs, the "improbable fictions" which hold our attention. The existence of these plays, constantly prompting debate and engaging us in their seemingly endless questioning and their capacity to elicit meaning, is central to the function of theatre in our society. It is not Shakespeare but his artefacts that are for "all time", or as much of that time as we continue to produce them and to be persuaded or provoked by them to talk, discuss and speculate. Drawing us in or allowing us to stay outside, enigmatic or explicit, these are indices of the indispensability of art and why Shakespeare matters.

Postscript: Romeo and Juliet (1595/6)

Romeo and Juliet is a much earlier tragedy than the others covered in this book but it crystallizes some of the issues discussed and the questions that have emerged. It is a tragedy in which individualistic illusions are crushed as well-meaning plans go wrong. It should be like a fairy story, where at the conclusion Romeo finds his Juliet, kisses her as she awakes and all is well. But that does not happen. He doesn't receive the message sent to him by the Friar so he knows nothing of the plot the Friar has hatched. He is deceived by events and kills himself, so when Juliet awakes and finds him dead, she takes her own life.

There is a fragility in the narrative which is dependent not on Romeo's character but on the events surrounding him and the environment in which he lives. Lines 1 and 3 of the Prologue explain the problem: "Two households, both alike in dignity,/ ... From ancient grudge break to new mutiny." This social enmity is historical and affects all levels of Veronese society in the play. Modern examples would be the conflict between the faith communities in Northern Ireland or different forms of Islam in the Middle East. The musical *West Side Story* (1957; filmed 1961), based on Shakespeare's play, portrayed it as a tension between two different ethnic gangs, the Sharks (Puerto Rican) and the Jets (Caucasian). At the centre of Shakespeare's play is a socio-political issue. What is the "ancient grudge" that caused the rift? The play provides no answer, but it begins with a demonstration of its consequences:

Abraham: *Do you bite your thumb at us, sir?*
Sampson: *I do bite my thumb, sir.*
Abraham: *Do you bite your thumb at us, sir?* (1.1.35–7)

At this point the action is playful and comic, although it turns serious when Tybalt arrives on the scene. But the play continues in comic vein with Romeo, who is a young, foolish lover apparently besotted with Rosaline. The first yearning of love has started to distance him from his 'gang', who regard the idea of going to the rival Capulets' masked ball as a prank. Romeo, despite his misgivings (1.4), is persuaded to go, partly to wean him off Rosaline (1.2.77–96). This happens when he sees Juliet; but the youthful prank turns into something serious, this time not between servants but between young members of the rival families.

Both Romeo and Juliet are love-struck but there is an innocence about the immediacy of their love. It promises to transcend the limits of the social context and the responsibilities that they have towards their warring families. At the end of the play, when Romeo and Juliet are both dead, Montague promises to erect a statue "in pure gold" (5.3.309) and Capulet reciprocates in a similar vein. But the irony is that, unlike in comedy where the younger generation marries, in Verona the older generation is left bereft of its children. The Duke in the play is the embodiment of the law but unable to control the violence that this historic grudge has produced. The lovers pay little heed to the potentially dangerous social situation in which they are enmeshed. The Church, represented by the Friar, meddles, and ultimately causes the deaths of the lovers. The Friar proposes solutions that rely on deceit and trickery, although he ascribes much of what he does to the opposing forces in 'Nature'. In Act 1, Juliet laments: "My only love sprung from my only hate!/Too early seen unknown, and known too late!" (1.4.261–2), but later Friar Laurence notes: "The earth that's nature's mother is her tomb:/What is her burying grave, that is her womb," (2.2.9–10), and he concludes:

> For nought so vile that on earth doth live
> But to the earth some special good doth give, ...
> Virtue itself turns vice, being misapplied,
> And vice sometime by action dignified. (2.2.17–8, 21–2)

This is manifested in *Macbeth* with the depiction of God's antithesis, the devil, represented by the weird sisters, whose "supernatural soliciting", Macbeth says, "Cannot be ill, cannot be good" (*Macbeth*, 1.3.140–1), but that is both "good" (he becomes Thane of Cawdor) and "ill" (it leads him to commit regicide); finally Macbeth's deceit is turned back on him in Malcolm's strategy to bring Birnam Wood to Dunsinane. In *Romeo and Juliet*, the Apothecary is seemingly the antithesis of the Friar, but he excuses his evil in giving the deadly poison to Romeo, claiming, "My poverty, but not my will, consents" (5.1.78).

The play brings together aspects that are apparent in both comedy and tragedy. The concept of the classical notion of tragedy is demonstrated, the rising action being in a comic frame but leading to the climax at the deaths of Mercutio and Tybalt in Act 3 Scene 1, after which Romeo cries out, "O, I am fortune's fool!" (3.1.123). It is as if the climax has changed the genre, setting the falling action towards the catastrophe firmly within the tragic. But the seeds of tragedy have been present from the start in the Prologue and underlying the initial 'playful' violence of the opening scene, although so it is in the opening of the comedies, which tend to begin with violence or threats of death. In this play the romantic comedy has to give way to tragedy, and almost to be in conflict with the tragedy that is to ensue. Romeo is warned by his friends about his interest in loving. Is the tragedy's cause "fortune", as Romeo claims, or the social context of hatred and political inability to sustain peace that frames the story?

The play was written in 1595/6, the same period as *A Midsummer Night's Dream*. In that comedy Puck uses a 'natural' potion at the command of the fairy king, Oberon. He mistakenly applies it to the eyelids of Lysander instead of Demetrius, and then to rectify the problem applies it to Demetrius's eyelids as well. The result is that both are now in love with Helena, while Hermia is abandoned. Comic mayhem is the result, until all is put right by order of Oberon. Meanwhile, he has made fun of his queen, Titania, by applying the love juice to her eyes and making her fall in love with the weaver Bottom, who he has turned into an ass. This is an aristocratic game in which the king of the fairies is in control, but once the joke has served its purpose Oberon can put it right because he has god-like power. In *Romeo and Juliet*, however, no one can put the problem right. There is no effective authority in Verona, political, spiritual or supernatural. Romeo and Juliet are victims of a social breakdown (a family feud) as much as their actions serve to intensify it. In youth and innocence, they believe they can rise above even their own identities, inscribed in their names, and the language that determines their being. So Juliet questions:

What's in a name? That which we call a rose
By any other word would smell as sweet. (2.1.90–1)

This is as naive about the social determination of identity and its foundation in language as Romeo's recourse to the Friar and what he represents. In this play the Church's power is seen to be ultimately ineffectual. The Friar, a traditional 'representative' of God, gets it wrong just like Puck, but without an Oberon to correct the error. The lovers are the victims of tragic coincidence since the message designed to bring them together safely is delayed because of the plague. Ironically, Mercutio dies crying out: "A plague o'both your houses!" (3.1.86), and so it turns out to be; he is a touchstone of the story. The venom of Mercutio's curse would have been apparent to Shakespeare's audience. Plague was a familiar experience for Londoners and not long before it had closed the theatres, or play 'houses', for an extended period.

Mercutio earlier ridicules Romeo for being in love, for being – in today's common parlance – 'away with the fairies'. His Queen Mab speech (1.4.55f.) parodies the fantasy in which he thinks Romeo is caught. Mercutio's speech gathers momentum to the point where it descends into an almost angry nonsense. Queen Mab is a figment of Mercutio's imagination: "Begot of nothing but vain fantasy,/Which is as thin of substance as the air/And more inconstant than the wind" (1.4.102–4), but Mercutio too will soon become "nothing", a victim of the hatred and conflict in the society in which he lives. His death is emblematic of the play as a whole and presaged the deeper conflicts in the four tragedies, where people are sacrificed in the context of forces that are beyond their capacity to control: princes, kings, generals, all of whom by their actions transgress the protocols of the societies in which they find themselves. In *Romeo and Juliet* the victims are not characters of high rank. They are young. They refuse to conform to their families' demands. Juliet refuses to marry Paris, defying the will of her father. And in doing so she violates an important, if extremely harsh, social decorum. As a consequence, Juliet dies.

In all of this Shakespeare doesn't condemn; he merely exposes the dilemma and leaves it for us, the audience, to come to our own conclusions. This postscript was written as the world commemorated the 100th anniversary of the start of the First World War, when the nationalistic ambitions of authoritarian aristocrats and self-centred politicians sent millions to their deaths, and at a time of religious conflict in the Middle East, displacing people and butchering individuals and communities for a 'cause'. What cause? "It is the cause, it is the cause, my soul:/Let me not name it to you, you chaste stars:/It is the cause" (*Othello*, 5.2.1–3). Cause can be a fabrication, a dishonestly contrived reaction, something far from the 'truth', from the immediacy of "Look, here comes a walking fire" expressed by the Fool in *King Lear* (3.4.93).

In its structure and the way it 'works' *Romeo and Juliet* is a different tragedy from the four plays discussed in this book. With the deaths of the two young lovers, Shakespeare produces a tragedy of a society that is out of control, in which hatred is fostered between two merchant families against the background of an impotent government and a meddling Church. *Romeo and Juliet* is not an 'innocent' play or a play about 'innocence', as some may be tempted to surmise. It is a play which structurally moves from an early comic narrative to a tragic one, raising as it does so the questions that Shakespeare asks in plays as seemingly different as *A Midsummer Night's Dream* and *Othello*. His questions are not confined by genre. As noted here and in *Shakespeare's Comedies*, two of his most challenging plays, *Twelfth Night* and *Hamlet*, were probably written in the same year and both are preoccupied with images of death. *Romeo and Juliet*, written possibly in the same year as *A Midsummer Night's Dream*, moves from the comedy of love to the tragedy of death, questioning aspects of an early modern culture that insists upon constructing identities for its subjects, and upon erecting lifeless statues that can contribute nothing to the future of society. As with the other plays considered in this book, it makes us think about what matters.

Ten technical terms

1 **Anagnorisis:** The moment of discovery or recognition.

2 **Catharsis:** A purging or release of emotions of pity and fear in the audience.

3 **Hamartia:** The fatal or tragic flaw within the protagonist, arising usually from an error of judgement or weakness of character.

4 **Hubris:** Excessive or outlandish pride, which in Greek tragedy tries the patience of the gods too far and leads to nemesis.

5 **Nemesis:** The retribution of the gods and the downfall caused by this.

6 **Pathos:** Stimulates pity or sorrow within the audience for the 'casualties' of the event; distinct from the downfall of the protagonist.

7 **Peripeteia:** A reversal of fortune leading to the downfall of the protagonist.

8 **Stichomythia:** Short, sharp dialogue, repartee or banter between characters, e.g. Hamlet and Gertrude in *Hamlet*, Act 3 Scene 4 lines 10–13.

9 **Pentameter:** The poetic line of five feet, each foot characterized by two stresses, e.g. iambus (soft/strong) or trochee (strong/soft). Shakespeare predominantly employed the iambic pentameter but he often varied both line length and the position of stresses for effect.

10 **Folio/quarto:** Book sizes in the 16th and 17th centuries, derived from the size of the paper used (*folio* is Latin

for 'leaf') and the number of times it was folded. For a folio edition, the standard sheet of paper (c.13.5 inches × 17 inches) was folded once, making two leaves or four pages. For a *quarto* the standard page was folded twice, making four leaves or eight pages. Quarto editions of some Shakespeare plays were published in his lifetime. The First Folio edition, containing most of his works, was published in 1623.

Ten '-isms'

11 **Catholicism:** Christianity provided a central authority, scholarship and a unifying influence in western Europe after the fall of the Roman Empire but the Church's increasing worldliness and abuses led to growing dissatisfaction by the 14th century. The Renaissance brought a re-examination of Christianity by humanists, although some (e.g. Erasmus, More) rejected reform when Luther and his supporters started to diverge from traditional teaching. The Roman Catholic Church initiated a movement (1545–63) to counter the Reformation, and papal authority was briefly re-instated in England in the reign of Mary I (1553–8).

12 **Humanism** is the general term for the renewed interest in classical ideas and literature that developed in Italian city-states during the 14th century and spread throughout Europe in the 15th and 16th centuries, helped by the invention of the printing press (c.1450). Inspired by a desire to access the knowledge of the ancient world, it emphasized the use of primary sources, encouraging intellectual curiosity and self-improvement. Humanists believed 'the new learning' created good Christians, good citizens and a deep appreciation of humankind and the created world. It changed European thought, leading to an expansion in the curricula of schools and universities. Its beliefs have been subsequently

modified by other ideologies, e.g. Christian humanism, liberal humanism etc.

13 **Protestantism** originated in the protest by Martin Luther, a German theologian in Wittenberg, who in 1517 attacked church practices he felt needed to be reformed. Luther's protest was inspired by the ideals of humanism. Protestantism based its authority not on tradition but on the Bible as the only source of truth, and placed much greater emphasis on the individual conscience. Protestantism soon divided into a number of denominations over differing theological emphases. In England, Henry VIII did not embrace Protestantism but seceded from papal authority to create an anglicized Catholic church of which he was the supreme head. A more Protestant theology was introduced under Edward VI and Elizabeth I, but elements of Catholic theology remained enshrined in Church of England doctrine, causing conflict with some forms of Protestantism, particularly Puritanism, in the reigns of Elizabeth I and the early Stuart monarchs.

14 **Romanticism** developed in the late 18th and early 19th centuries. It regarded art and literature in the context of its 'organic nature', developing from laws within itself. It looked towards the ideal, found in myths and also in the innocence of ordinary people expressed in simplicity of language, and rejected the neoclassism of the 18th century. For the Romantics, Shakespeare's art came from his "natural genius", a view advocated particularly by Coleridge.

15 **Realism** reacted against the Romantic notion of the ideal, the realist novelists of the 19th century, e.g. Dickens, depicting as clearly as possible what they considered to be the realities and experiences of life in all strata of society. It is a mimetic form which transferred onto the stage with the works of Ibsen in particular. Realism influenced dramatic criticism in a concentration on character as if the character in the play actually existed.

16 **Archetypal Criticism** grew out of Jungian psychology in the early 20th century, taking realistic and psychological aspects of Shakespearean criticism into a new dimension. Primordial myths within the collective unconsciousness were present in and could be aroused by a variety of differing texts; e.g. *Hamlet* should be read in the context of Aeschylus' or Sophocles' work, which would reveal similar archetypal modes in characters such as Orestes and Oedipus in mother/son relationships and in a concentration on incest and on the retribution of the gods. Through psychology Archetypal Criticism is also linked with the classical concept of catharsis.

17 **Modernism** rejected the 19th century concept of the 'organic nature' of art, and in the early 20th century also rejected realism. Modernist writers, e.g. James Joyce and Virginia Woolf, made the reader aware that they were 'reading' something which had been 'written', thereby detaching the reader. In the theatre, Modernist-influenced movements, such as constructivism, arose at about the same time as Communism and the Russian Revolution. In Germany they were followed by the politically orientated theatre of Bertolt Brecht, although Modernism was not overtly political and also had exponents on the right, e.g. Ezra Pound.

18 **Post-Modernism** arose out of Modernism and the experience of a war-torn Europe, which led to the rejection of authority by some. Like Modernism, it rejected the linearity of an artistic product and worked through presenting patterns of experience which did not have to express a 'sense of meaning'. It conveyed thereby a vacuity of existence and absence of purpose, exemplified in drama by Beckett's *Waiting for Godot*.

19 **New Historicism** questions contemporary interpretations which look for the 'relevance' of drama, insisting that Shakespeare can be understood only by being located within the period of the plays' inception and composition. This approach draws on historical evidence from outside the text, including sources not necessarily connected with the text, e.g. medical cases, tax records etc.

20 **Cultural Materialism** attempts to understand the 'materiality' of the work of art within the context of its historical production and location. It denies the universality of truths contained within the text but not that texts are devoid of meaning: texts do not mean in themselves but have meanings conferred upon them. Cultural Materialism fills the vacuity of meaning with an overtly stated ideological understanding of material reality. It draws heavily on the philosophies of writers such as Raymond Williams, Derrida, Foucault and Althusser.

Ten(+) Elizabethan/Jacobean dramatists

21 **Thomas Kyd** (1558–94). Known for *The Spanish Tragedy* (1589?).

22 **Christopher Marlowe** (1564–93). Among his plays are *Tamburlaine the Great*, *Dr Faustus*, *The Jew of Malta*, *Edward II*. One of the 'University Wits', with **John Lyly** (1553–1606), **George Peele** (1558–96) and **Robert Greene** (1558–92).

23 **Thomas Dekker** (1570–1632). Known for *The Shoemaker's Holiday* (1599) and collaborating with Thomas Middleton on *The Honest Whore* (1604) and *The Roaring Girl* (1604) and with John Webster on *Westward Ho!* (1604).

24 **Ben Jonson** (1572–1637). Wrote numerous plays, including *Everyman in His Humour* (1598), *Everyman Out of His Humour* (1599), *Volpone* (1605), *The Alchemist* (1610), *The Devil is an Ass* (1616).

25 **John Marston** (1576–1634). Satiric poet and dramatist whose plays include *Antonio and Mellida* (1599), *Antonio's Revenge* (1599), *The Dutch Courtesan* (1603/4), *The*

Malcontent (1604). He collaborated with Jonson and **George Chapman** (*c.*1560–1634) on *Eastward Ho!* (1605).

26 **Thomas Middleton** (1580–1627). Probably collaborated with Shakespeare on *Macbeth*. Among his numerous plays are *The Roaring Girl* (1610) with Dekker, *A Chaste Maid in Cheapside* (1611) and *The Changeling* (1622) with **William Rowley** (1585–1626), and possibly *The Revenger'sTragedy* (1606/7), often attributed to **Cyril Tourneur** (1575–1626), author of *The Atheist's Tragedy* (1607–11?).

27 **John Webster** (*c.*1580–*c.*1634). Known in particular for *The White Devil* (1612) and *The Duchess of Malfi* (1613/14).

28 **Philip Massinger** (1583–1640). Prolific playwright who collaborated with several contemporaries; probably best known for *A New Way to Pay Old Debts* (1621/2) and *The Roman Actor* (1626).

29 **Francis Beaumont** (1584–1616) and **John Fletcher** (1579–1625) worked together from 1605/6 to *c.*1613, when Beaumont retired. Their plays include *Philaster* (pre-1610), *The Maid's Tragedy* (pre-1611), *A King and No King* (1611). Beaumont wrote *The Knight of the Burning Pestle* (1607). Fletcher collaborated with Shakespeare on *Henry VIII* (1613) and with Massinger and others.

30 **John Ford** (1586–*c.*1640). Worked with Dekker and Rowley on *The Witch of Edmonton* (1621). His plays include *Perkin Warbeck* (1622?), *The Broken Heart* (1627), *'Tis Pity She's a Whore* (1629) and *Love's Sacrifice* (1632).

20(+) renowned Shakespearean actors

This is a personal selection of living British actors renowned for their Shakespearean performances on stage and/

or film. (Note: Renowned actors of previous eras are listed in a companion volume in this series, *Shakespeare's Comedies*.)

31 Ian McKellen (b. 1939). One of the UK's finest tragic actors, known particularly for Macbeth (RSC, 1976), his Iago to Willard White's Othello (RSC, 1989), King Lear (RSC, 2007) and his fascistic Richard III (National Theatre, 1990).

32 Derek Jacobi (b. 1938). A major stage and screen actor since starring in *I, Claudius* in the 1970s. His Hamlet (Prospect Company, 1977) was both emotionally and intellectually strong and influenced later interpretations, including Branagh's, and he gave a moving King Lear (London, 2010).

33 Kenneth Branagh (b. 1960). Renowned for bringing Shakespeare to mass audiences with film adaptations of *Henry V* (1989), *Much Ado About Nothing* (1993), *Hamlet* (1996), *Love's Labour's Lost* (2000) and *As You Like It* (2006). His Hamlet (RSC, 1992) and Henry V (RSC 1984) are amongst his most respected stage work, influencing his films.

34 Ian Holm (b. 1931). Developed through the RSC's early years in numerous Shakespearean roles, including Romeo and Hamlet, but probably best known for his King Lear (National, 1998).

35 Jonathan Pryce (b. 1947). A player of many Shakespearean roles, known particularly for his tour de force as Hamlet (Royal Court, 1980); his King Lear (Almeida, 2012) displayed a similar intensity of pain and torment.

36 Antony Sher (b. 1949). A highly accomplished actor in Shakespearean and Elizabethan works, most notably as the Fool to Gambon's Lear (1982), Titus Andronicus (1994), Macbeth (1999) and Malevole in Marston's *The Malcontent* (2002). His spider-like Richard III on crutches (1984) was characteristic of his challenging style.

37 **Mark Rylance** (b. 1960). Became the first artistic director of the Globe Theatre in 1995, restoring historicity to productions and establishing its reputation. Has also performed major roles with the RSC, notably an acclaimed pyjama-clad Hamlet, the night attire symbolizing his 'madness'.

38 **Alan Howard** (b. 1937). An RSC stalwart from 1966 to 1983, excelling as Oberon and Theseus, *A Midsummer Night's Dream* (1970), Richard II, Henry V, Hamlet and Coriolanus with his command of the language and great stage presence.

39 **Jonathan Slinger** (b. 1972). Has worked at the National Theatre, the Globe Theatre and the RSC, where he was prominent in Michael Boyd's production of the history plays and as Macbeth (2011) and a memorable Hamlet (2013).

40 **David Tennant** (b. 1971). One of his generation's leading Shakespearean actors, and particularly praised for his Hamlet (2008) and Richard II (2013), although better known as the tenth Dr Who.

41 **Patrick Stewart** (b. 1940). Starring in *Star Trek* interrupted the stage career of one of the UK's principal Shakespearean actors. He returned to the RSC as Prospero, *The Tempest* (2006) and Antony to Harriet Walter's Cleopatra. In 2008 he was a strong Claudius to Tennant's energetic Hamlet.

42 **Simon Russell Beale** (b. 1961). One of the intellects of the modern stage, he has developed strong working relationships with directors, particularly Sam Mendes who directed him as Richard III and Ariel, *The Tempest* (RSC, 1992/3), and as King Lear (National, 2014).

43 **Rory Kinnear** (b. 1978). An intelligent, no-nonsense actor who has impressed particularly as Hamlet (National, 2010) and as Iago to Adrian Lester's Othello (National, 2014).

44 **Jude Law** (b. 1972). A film and stage actor who played Hamlet at Elsinore in 2009 in a Donmar Warehouse transfer. Has played the title role in Marlowe's *Dr Faustus* and Giovanni in Ford's *'Tis Pity She's a Whore*, and most recently Henry V (London, 2012).

45 **David Warner** (b. 1941). The Hamlet of the 'Angry Young Man' generation in the famous Peter Hall production (1965), he has had a long and distinguished career, latterly playing King Lear (Chichester, 2005) and Falstaff (RSC, 2007).

46 **Ben Kingsley** (b. 1943). Famed for his film depiction of Ghandi (1982), he had already enjoyed a distinguished stage career, strongly influenced by working in Brook's famous *A Midsummer Night's Dream* (1970). He has played Hamlet (1975) and Othello (1985) for the RSC.

47 **Adrian Lester** (b. 1968). Played Othello with Kinnear as Iago (National, 2013). His career was influenced by the radical Cheek by Jowl company, for which he played Rosalind in the 1991 all-male production of *As You Like It*.

48 **Timothy West** (b. 1934) and **Sam West** (b. 1966). Father Timothy, one of the elder statesmen of the British stage, has worked with the RSC and the touring Prospect Theatre Company playing roles including Macbeth and King Lear, and Claudius to Jacobi's Hamlet. Sam has played roles for the National Theatre and the RSC, including Hamlet (2001).

49 **Toby Stephens** (b. 1969). Son of the late Robert Stephens, whose King Lear (RSC, 1993) was much admired, and Maggie Smith. Has been acclaimed particularly for his Coriolanus (RSC, 1994) and Hamlet (RSC, 2004).

50 **Michael Gambon** (b. 1940). A highly respected actor who has played many of Shakespeare's most well-known roles, including Othello, Macbeth, Coriolanus, King Lear (RSC, 1982) and Falstaff in *Henry IV*, Parts 1 and 2 (National, 2005).

20(+) renowned Shakespearean actresses

This is a personal selection of living British actresses renowned for their Shakespearean performances on stage and/or film. (Note: Renowned actresses of previous eras are listed in a companion volume in this series, *Shakespeare's Comedies*.)

51 **Judi Dench** (b. 1934). One of the UK's most renowned actresses, especially for her Shakespearean performances, her Lady Macbeth to McKellen's Macbeth (1976) being a particular triumph. Later television and film roles have included M in the James Bond films and Queen Elizabeth in *Shakespeare in Love*.

52 **Fiona Shaw** (b. 1958). Has worked extensively with the RSC and the National Theatre, playing major female roles in *As You Like It*, *The Taming of the Shrew*, *Much Ado About Nothing* and also the title role in *Richard II* in 1995.

53 **Maggie Smith** (b. 1934). One of the most famous actresses of the day, establishing herself in major Shakespearean productions – particularly notable was her Desdemona opposite Olivier's Othello (National, 1960; filmed 1965) – as well as in film and television.

54 **Emma Thompson** (b. 1959). A leading actress in film and theatre, responsible with former husband Kenneth Branagh for a renaissance of Shakespeare in film. Particularly memorable was her portrayal of Beatrice in the film of *Much Ado About Nothing* (1993).

55 **Cherie Lunghi** (b. 1952). A distinguished actress with the RSC in the 1970s, playing Cordelia, *King Lear* (1977), Viola, *Twelfth Night* and appearing in *The Winter's Tale*, *Much Ado About Nothing* and *As You Like It*.

56 **Janet Suzman** (b. 1939). Leading female roles in many Shakespearean plays from the 1960s onwards include Portia, *The Merchant of Venice*, Ophelia, *Hamlet*, Kate, *The Taming of the Shrew*, Beatrice, *Much Ado About Nothing*, Rosalind, *As You Like It*; renowned for her Cleopatra opposite Richard Johnson's Antony (RSC, 1972/3; televised, 1974). In 2007 she played Volumnia, *Coriolanus* at Stratford.

57 **Juliet Stevenson** (b. 1956). Well-known theatre, television and film actress who in the late 1970s and 1980s played Isabella, *Measure for Measure*, Cressida, *Troilus and Cressida* and Rosalind, *As You Like It* with the RSC.

58 **Harriet Walter** (b. 1950). Portrayed Lady Macbeth to Sher's Macbeth (1999) in one of the great productions of recent years. Has played Helena, *All's Well That Ends Well*, Viola, *Twelfth Night*, Imogen, *Cymbeline* and many other roles, including Brutus in the 2013 all-female production of *Julius Caesar*.

59 **Sinead Cusack** (b. 1948) and **Niamh Cusack** (b. 1959). Sinead has played many female Shakespearean roles, including Beatrice opposite Jacobi's Benedick (1982–4) in one of the great pairings for *Much Ado About Nothing* in the modern theatre. Sister Niamh's Shakespearean roles include Desdemona to Kingsley's Othello (RSC, 1985) and Juliet in 1986.

60 **Zoë Wanamaker** (b. 1949). Actress of stage, film and television and daughter of Sam Wanamaker, the force behind London's reconstructed Globe Theatre. She played Beatrice to Russell Beale's Benedick (National) and has appeared in *The Taming of the Shrew*, *Twelfth Night*, *Comedy of Errors* and *Othello*.

61 **Penelope Wilton** (b. 1946). A successful stage and screen actress, in 1970 she played Regan to Michael Hordern's Lear (Nottingham) and Desdemona in the BBC television production of *Othello*, and gave one of the most comic portrayals of Beatrice in an unforgettable production of *Much Ado About Nothing* (National Theatre, 1981).

62 **Vanessa Redgrave** (b. 1937). Has taken major roles in many Shakespeare productions since the late 1950s, when she appeared as Helena, *A Midsummer Night's Dream*. More recently she played Beatrice opposite James Earl Jones as Benedick in *Much Ado About Nothing* (Old Vic, 2013).

63 **Helen Mirren** (b. 1945). Came to prominence with her Cleopatra for the National Youth Theatre, after which she joined the RSC, playing roles such as Cressida, *Troilus and Cressida*, Ophelia, *Hamlet* and Queen Margaret, *Henry VI*, Parts 1, 2 and 3. Now famous for her many television and film roles.

64 **Imogen Stubbs** (b. 1961). Known for her Desdemona opposite the opera singer Willard White's Othello (RSC, 1989; televised 1990) and her Viola in the film version of *Twelfth Night* (1996).

65 **Frances de la Tour** (b. 1944). Came to prominence for her comic portrayal of Helena in Brook's production of *A Midsummer Night's Dream*. Played Cleopatra to Alan Bates' Antony (RSC, 1999) and the title role in an all-female promenade production of *Hamlet* (Half Moon, 1979).

66 **Frances Barber** (b. 1958). Has played many leading Shakespearean roles, including Goneril to McKellen's King Lear in Trevor Nunn's stage production (RSC, 2007) and subsequent Channel 4 TV film (2008).

67 **Lindsay Duncan** (b. 1950). Played Helen of Troy, *Troilus and Cressida* (RSC, 1985) and Hippolyta and Titania, *A Midsummer Night's Dream* (RSC, 1995), a production which transferred to New York and then was adapted for television. In 2012 she played the Duchess of York in BBC2's *Richard II* with Ben Whishaw as the king.

68 **Barbara Leigh Hunt** (b. 1935). Portrayed many Shakespearean roles in the 1970s and 1980s, including Goneril, *King Lear*, Queen Margaret, *Richard III*, Paulina, *The Winter's Tale*, Mistress Ford, *The Merry Wives of Windsor* and Gertrude, *Hamlet*, the last a portrayal in which the audience never quite knew whether she could see the Ghost or not.

69 **Josette Simon** (b. 1960). Well-known for her television performances but has also worked with the RSC and the National Theatre, including as one of the 'weird sisters', *Macbeth* (RSC, 1982), Iras, *Antony and Cleopatra* (RSC, 1983), Margaret, *Much Ado About Nothing* (RSC, 1982–4) and Hippolyta and Titania, *A Midsummer Night's Dream* (RSC, 1999).

70 **Penny Downie** (b. 1954). An accomplished stage and television actress who has played many of the main female roles for the RSC, including Lady Capulet, *Romeo and Juliet* (1984), Hermione and Perdita, *The Winter's Tale* (1986), Hippolyta and Titania, *A Midsummer Night's Dream* (1984) Lady Anne to Sher's Richard III (1984); and Gertrude to Tennant's Hamlet (2008; television, 2009).

Ten(+) film/TV/DVD productions

71 **Hamlet** (1948); directed by Laurence Olivier, with Olivier in the title role. Contrast this with the 1964 Russian version directed by Grigori Kozintsev.

72 **Hamlet** (1990); directed by Franco Zeffirelli, with Mel Gibson (Hamlet), Glenn Close (Gertrude); Alan Bates (Claudius), and Helena Bonham Carter (Ophelia). Compare this with Kenneth Branagh's 1996 film version, with Branagh in the title role, Julie Christie, Derek Jacobi and Kate Winslet.

73 **King Lear** (1971); directed by Peter Brook, based on his 1962 Stratford production, with Paul Scofield as King Lear. Compare this with Grigori Kozintsev's 1970 Russian film version.

74 **King Lear** (1982); part of the BBC TV Shakespeare series, directed by Jonathan Miller, with Michael Hordern (King Lear) and Frank Middlemass (the Fool). The BBC/WGBH-Boston Masterpiece Theatre DVD (1998) is a recording of the National Theatre's 1997 production, directed by Richard Eyre, with Ian Holm (King Lear), Timothy West (Gloucester) and Michael Bryant (the Fool).

75 **Macbeth** (1971); directed by Roman Polanski, with Jon Finch (Macbeth) and Francesca Annis (Lady Macbeth). Also available on DVD is the Globe Theatre's 2014 production, directed by Eve Best, with Joseph Millson (Macbeth) and Samantha Spiro (Lady Macbeth).

76 **Macbeth** (1978/9); a Thames TV adaptation, directed by Philip Carson, of Trevor Nunn's 1976–8 RSC production with Ian McKellen (Macbeth) and Judi Dench (Lady Macbeth). Compare this with the BBC 4 TV production directed by Rupert Goold, adapted from his 2007 Chichester Festival Theatre production, with Patrick Stewart (Macbeth) and Kate Fleetwood (Lady Macbeth).

77 **Othello** (1965); directed by Stuart Burge, of John Dexter's staging of the 1964–66 National Theatre production, with Laurence Olivier (Othello), Frank Finlay (Iago) and Maggie Smith (Desdemona).

78 **Othello** (1995). A US/UK film directed by Oliver Parker, with Laurence Fishburne (Othello) and Kenneth Branagh (Iago).

79 **Othello** (1981); part of the BBC TV Shakespeare series, directed by Jonathan Miller, with Anthony Hopkins (Othello), Bob Hoskins (Iago) and Penelope Wilton (Desdemona).

80 Romeo and Juliet (1968); directed by Franco Zeffirelli, with Leonard Whiting (Romeo) and Olivia Hussey (Juliet). See also the contemporized film version (1996) directed by Baz Luhrman, with Leonardo DiCaprio and Claire Danes, and Julian Fellowes' freely adapted screenplay in an Italian Renaissance setting, directed by Carlo Carlei (2013), with Douglas Booth and Hailee Steinfeld.

20 Questions

81 Who wrote the *Poetics*?

82 Name Hamlet's father.

83 What flowers does Ophelia say "withered all when my father died"?

84 According to the Gravedigger (First Clown), why was Hamlet sent to England?

85 Name the bird which inhabits Macbeth's castle?

86 How old does King Lear say he is?

87 Name Iago's wife.

88 Hamlet asks the players to perform *The Murder of Gonzago* but what name does Hamlet later give to the play?

89 Name the three daughters of King Lear.

90 In *King Lear*, which of Gloucester's sons is illegitimate?

91 In the bad Quarto of *Hamlet* (1603), the father of Laertes and Ophelia is known as Corambis. What is his name in Q2 and the First Folio?

92 Who sings the 'willow song' in *Othello*?

93 *The Malcontent* was probably first performed in the same year as *Hamlet*. Who wrote it?

94 What is *anagnorisis*?

95 Who is Romeo's first love?

96 In *King Lear*, what name does Edgar assume when he escapes to the heath?

97 Who bids farewell to the "Pride, pomp and circumstance of glorious war!"?

98 According to Mercutio in *Romeo and Juliet*, who is the "fairies' midwife"?

99 What are the three unities?

100 Which playwright probably collaborated with Shakespeare on *Macbeth*?

Notes

Publication details are not given here for titles listed in Suggested further reading.

1 H. Northrop Frye, *The Anatomy of Criticism* (Princeton: Princeton University Press, 1957).

2 Aristotle, *Poetics*, p. 10.

3 A. C. Bradley, *Shakespearean Tragedy* (London, 1906).

4 Aristotle, op. cit, p.11.

5 Ibid, p. 11.

6 L. C. Knights, 'How Many Children had Lady Macbeth?' (1933), *A Shakespeare Reader: Sources and Criticism*.

7 L. C. Knights, *Drama and Society in the Age of Jonson* (London: Chatto & Windus, 1937).

8 Stephen Greenblatt, *Renaissance Self-Fashioning: From More to Shakespeare* (Chicago: Chicago University Press, 1980), p. 5.

9 Jonathan Dollimore, *Radical Tragedy*, p. 153.

10 *Shakespearean Tragedy* (ed. J. Drakakis) provides arguments against the traditional humanist or Christian interpretations of tragedy in literary criticism; Drakakis' introduction proves an important survey of the radical Marxist interpretations of tragedy and their questioning of Liberal Humanist positions. Counter-arguments from the Liberal Humanist position are found in Brian Vickers' *Appropriating Shakespeare: Contemporary Critical Quarrels* (New Haven and London: Yale University Press, 1993). Kiernan Ryan's *Shakespeare* (Basingstoke: Palgrave, 3rd edn, 2002) provides a perspective which, with a directness and lucidity of style, tackles critics of any ideological persuasion who might try to place Shakespeare within a conservative political orthodoxy or dimension.

11 *The Tragicall Historie of Hamlet Prince of Denmarke, 1603* (Edinburgh: Edinburgh University Press, 1966), p. 28.

12 Eleanor Prosser, *Hamlet and Revenge* (Stanford, CA: Stanford University Press, 1967).

13 John Drakakis (ed.), *Alternative Shakespeares* (London: Methuen, 1985) p. 2.

14 Ibid, p. 4.

15 Michael Scott, 'Hamlet, Castiglione and the Renaissance Courtier', *History and Culture* (1998), vol. 4, pp 29–38.

16 P.O. Kristeller, *Renaissance Thought*, p. 20f.

17 *The RSC Shakespeare: Complete Works*, p. 2002, lines 170–184.

18 Baldassare Castiglione, *The Book of the Courtier*, trans. Sir Thomas Hoby, 1561; ed. J. H. Whitfield (London: Dent, 1974), pp 95-6.

19 Castiglione, *The Book of the Courtier*, trans. G. Bull, p. 351, note 4.

20 Ibid, quoting from Plutarch's *Rise and Fall of Athens: Nine Greek Lives*, trans. Ian Scott-Kilvert.

21 *The RSC Shakespeare: Complete Works*, pp 2001–2, lines 105–39.

22 Jean Calvin, *The Institution of Christian Religion* (1535), trans. Thomas Norton, 1561; reprinted London, 1599. See Robin Headlam Wells, *Shakespeare, Politics and The State* (London: Macmillan, 1986), pp 118–19.

23 David Scott Kastan, *A Will to Believe: Shakespeare and Religion*, pp 126–7.

24 John Marston, *The Malcontent*, ed. M. L. Wine (London: Edward Arnold, 1965), 4.5.91–2.

25 Scott Kastan, op.cit., p. 3.

26 O. B. Hardison, Jnr, *Christian Rite and Christian Drama in the Middle Ages*.

27 Drakakis, *Shakespearean Tragedy*, pp 388–9.

28 Michael Scott, 'Letters on *King Lear*' (*Critical Survey*, I.I.1989), pp 10–16.

29 Ibid, pp 12–13.

30 Line 264 has 'howl, howl, howl' in the First Folio; other editions have a fourth 'howl'.

31 Graham Martin and Stephen Regan, *Shakespeare: Texts and Contexts* (ed. K. Ryan), p. 262.

32 Knights, 'How Many Children had Lady Macbeth?', *A Shakespeare Reader: Sources and Criticism*, pp. 115-29.

33 Ibid, pp 117.

34 Ibid, p. 118.

35 Ibid, p. 117.

36 Ibid, p. 124.

37 Jan Kott, *Shakespeare Our Contemporary*, pp 68-9.

38 E. M. W. Tillyard, *The Elizabethan World Picture* (London: Chatto & Windus, 1943), and *Shakespeare's History Plays* (London: Chatto & Windus, 1944).

39 E. A. J. Honigmann, *Shakespeare: The 'Lost Years'* (Manchester: Manchester University Press, 1985).

40 Scott Kastan, op. cit., p. 39.

41 Alan Sinfield, in *A Shakespeare Reader: Sources and Criticism*, p. 130.

42 Ibid, p. 136.

43 Gordon Williams, *Macbeth, Text and Performance* series, p. 10.

44 Ibid, p. 9.

45 Thomas de Quincey, 'On the Knocking on the Gate in *Macbeth*' (1823) in *De Quincey as Critic*.

46 Malcolm Evans, *Signifying Nothing: Truth's True Contents in Shakespeare's Text* (Brighton: Harvester Press, 1986), p. 117.

47 Neil MacGregor, *Shakespeare's Restless World*, pp 175-89.

48 Ibid, p. 183.

49 Julia Briggs, *This Stage-Play World: Texts and Contexts, 1580-1625* (Oxford: Oxford University Press, 2nd edn, 1997), pp 94-9.

50 Ibid, p. 96.

51 Edward Bond, *Plays: 2* (Lond: Eyre Methuen, 1978), author's preface to *Lear*, p.3.

52 The spelling 'Rodorigo' is used in the First Folio; some other editions use the spelling 'Roderigo'.

53 Bernard Spivack, *Shakespeare and the Allegory of Evil*.

54 Martin Wine, *Othello: Text and Performance* series, pp 32–3.

55 Greenblatt, op. cit., p. 238.

56 Wine, op. cit., pp 31–2.

57 Catherine Belsey, *Shakespeare and the Loss of Eden*, pp 14–15.

58 William Empson, 'Honest in Othello', in *The Structure of Complex Words* (London: Chatto & Windus, 1951).

59 Wine, op. cit., p. 66.

60 Frank Marcus, *The Sunday Telegraph*, 12 September 1971.

61 Greenblatt, op. cit., pp 236–7.

62 Wine, op. cit. p. 35.

63 E. A. J. Honigmann, *Shakespeare: Seven Tragedies*, p. 56.

Suggested further reading

Books suggested as further reading in *Shakespeare's Comedies* are not included here but many are also appropriate to the Shakespearean tragedies.

Aristotle (trans. M. Heath), *Poetics* (London: Penguin, 1996)

Belsey, C., *Shakespeare and the Loss of Eden: The Construction of Family Values in Early Modern Culture* (Basingstoke: Macmillan, 1999)

Bennet, S., *Performing Nostalgia: Shifting Shakespeare and the Contemporary Past* (London and New York: Routledge, 1996)

Bentley, E. (ed.), *The Theory of the Modern Stage* (Harmondsworth: Penguin, 1976)

Boal, A. (trans. C. A. and M. O. Leal McBride), *Theater of the Oppressed* (London: Pluto Press, 1979)

Bradley, A. C., *Shakespearean Tragedy* (Basingstoke: Macmillan, 3rd revised edn, 1992)

Brecht, B. (trans. J. Willett), *Brecht on Theatre* (London: Methuen, 1964)

Brown, R. D. and Johnson, D. (eds.), *A Shakespeare Reader: Sources and Criticism* (Basingstoke: Macmillan in association with the Open University, 2000)

Castiglione, B. (trans. G. Bull), *The Book of the Courtier* (Harmondsworth: Penguin, 1967)

De Quincey, T., 'On the Knocking on the Gate in *Macbeth*' (1823), in *De Quincey as Critic*, ed. J. E. Jordan (London: Routledge, 1973), pp. 240–4, or in the Casebook series' *Shakespeare: Macbeth*, ed. J. Wain (London: Macmillan, 1969), pp 90–3.

Dollimore, J., *Radical Tragedy* (New York and London: Harvester Wheatsheaf, 2nd edn, 1989)

Suggested further reading

Drakakis, J. (ed.), *Shakespearean Tragedy* (London: Longman, 1992)

Greenblatt, S., *Renaissance Self-Fashioning: From More to Shakespeare* (Chicago: Chicago University Press, 1980).

Hardison Jnr, O. B., *Christian Rite and Christian Drama in the Middle Ages* (Baltimore, MD: Johns Hopkins Press, 1965).

Hawthorn, J., *Cunning Passages: New Historicism, Cultural Materialism and Marxism in the Contemporary Literary Debate* (London: Edward Arnold, 1996)

Honigmann, E. A. J., *Shakespeare: Seven Tragedies: The Dramatist's Manipulation of Response* (Basingstoke: Macmillan, 1976)

Jardine, L., *Reading Shakespeare Historically* (London and New York: Routledge, 1996)

Kastan, D. Scott, *A Will to Believe: Shakespeare and Religion* (Oxford: Oxford University Press, 2014)

Kott, J. (trans. B. Taborski), *Shakespeare Our Contemporary* (London: Methuen, revised edn, 1967)

Kristeller, P. O., *Renaissance Thought* (New York: Harper Row, 1961)

MacGregor, N., *Shakespeare's Restless World* (London: Allen Lane, 2012)

Machiavelli, N. (trans. G. Bull), *The Prince* (London: Penguin, 1961)

Pfister, M. (trans. J. Halliday), *The Theory and Analysis of Drama* (Cambridge: Cambridge University Press, 1988)

Ross, J. B. and McLaughlin, M. M. (eds.), *The Portable Renaissance Reader* (Harmondsworth: Penguin, 1977)

Ryan, K. (ed.), *Shakespeare: Texts and Contexts* (Basingstoke: Macmillan in association with the Open University, 2000)

Scott, M. (gen. ed.), *Text and Performance* series (Basingstoke: Macmillan): Peter Davison, *Hamlet* (1983); Gordon Williams, *Macbeth* (1985); Gamini Salgãdo, *King Lear* (1984); Martin Wine, *Othello* (1984); Peter Holding, *Romeo and Juliet* (1992).

Scott, M. (gen. ed.), *The Critics Debate* series (Basingstoke: Macmillan): Michael Hattaway, *Hamlet* (1987); Peter Davison, *Othello* (1988); Ann Thompson, *King Lear* (1988).

Spivack, B., *Shakespeare and the Allegory of Evil* (New York and London: Columbia University Press, 1958)

Stanislavsky, C. (trans. E. R. Hapgood), *An Actor Prepares* (London: Geoffrey Bles, 1937)

Stanislavsky, C. (trans. E. R. Hapgood), *Building a Character* (London: Methuen, 1968)

Willett, J., *The Theatre of Bertolt Brecht* (London: Eyre Methuen, 1977)

Wilson Knight, G., *The Wheel of Fire* (London: Methuen, 4th revised edn, 1967)

Answers to 20 Questions

81 Aristotle.

82 King Hamlet, or Old Hamlet.

83 Violets [4.4.185–6].

84 Because he is mad (5.1.114).

85 The martlet (1.6.5).

86 Over 80 (4.6.63–4).

87 Emilia.

88 The Mousetrap.

89 Goneril, Regan, Cordelia.

90 Edmund.

91 Polonius.

92 Desdemona [4.3.43–59].

93 John Marston.

94 The moment of discovery or recognition.

95 Rosaline.

96 Poor Tom.

97 Othello (3.3.392).

98 Queen Mab [1.4.55–6].

99 Time, place, action.

100 Thomas Middleton.

Acknowledgements

This book would not have been possible without the help, support and love of my wife, Eirlys, to whom I owe more gratitude than I can express. I'm also grateful for the support of our daughters and their husbands and our grandchildren, who ensure we get our priorities right. My thanks go to my friend and colleague John Drakakis for kindly reading through the draft version of the book, editing and making incisive comments and suggestions, many of which have informed or been incorporated into the text. I owe thanks to my literary agent Charlotte Howard, to my publisher Iain Campbell, and my publishing editor Hilary Marsden, for their patience and encouragement. I am, of course, grateful to scholars I've known and to Shakespearean scholarship and theatrical performances over the years which have informed this book in so many ways.

Picture credits

The author and publisher would like to give their thanks for permission to use the following images:

Fortune and Her Wheel: illustration from vol. 1 of Boccaccio's *De Casibus Virorum Illustrium* (1467; Glasgow; Glasgow University Library)

Hamlet (Chapter 2) © Rex/Donald Cooper

King Lear © Rex/Donald Cooper

Macbeth © Rex/Alastair Muir

Othello © Rex/Alastair Muir

Hamlet (Chapter 6) © Rex/Geraint Lewis

Index

ALL THAT MATTERS: SHAKESPEARE'S TRAGEDIES

All That Matters books are written by the world's leading experts, to introduce the most exciting and relevant areas of an important topic to students and general readers.

From Bioethics to Muhammad and Philosophy to Sustainability, the All That Matters series covers the most controversial and engaging topics from science, philosophy, history, religion and other fields. The authors are world-class academics or top public intellectuals, on a mission to bring the most interesting and challenging areas of their subject to new readers.

Each book contains a unique '100 Ideas' section, giving inspiration to readers whose interest has been piqued and who want to explore the subject further. Find out more at:

www.allthatmattersbooks.com
Facebook/allthatmattersbooks
Twitter@All_That_Matters